KEYS TO A HAPPY LIFE:
THE BEATITUDES ACCORDING TO JESUS

KEYS TO A HAPPY LIFE:
THE BEATITUDES ACCORDING TO JESUS

Michael L. Faber

Elk Grove Publications

Elk Grove, CA

Copyright ©2014 Michael L. Faber

All rights reserved. No part of this publication may be reproduced or distributed in any form or by any means, electronic or mechanical, without prior permission in writing from the publisher.

Requests for permission to make copies of any part of this work should be sent to the author at mfaber@elkgrove.net, subject line "permissions." Publisher hereby grants permission to reviewers to quote up to 100 words from up to three works in their reviews, and requests that hyperlinks to said reviews be emailed to the address above or physical copies mailed to the address below.

ISBN-13: 978-1-940781-07-5
Elk Grove Publications
9124 Elk Grove Blvd.
Elk Grove, CA 95624
United States of America

Cover photo ©James Steidl, 123RF.com
ID#7059096 All rights reserved.

Printed in United States of America

INTRODUCTION

Keys to a Happy Life:
The Beatitudes According to Jesus

These days, everyone wants to be happy. Recognition of the individual quest for happiness has been a big driving force for social change in the 21st century. There are many paths to happiness. There is the direct approach, which is much in favor these days. If something makes *you* happy, just do it. Don't worry about social conventions or the sensibilities or rights of others, *you* deserve to be happy. If others cared about you, they would want *you* to be happy. God wants *you* to be happy. Therefore, any of His teachings or rules that stand in the way of *your* happiness are probably misinterpreted or outmoded, and are justifiably ignored.

This direct approach to happiness is much in vogue in the 21st Century Western World. It started with the Disney movies of the 1990s where the theme was, "just follow your heart," and moved on with power to the egotistical, self-centered world we now find ourselves. The public seems to have bought the concept that everyone should be happy. Of course, not everyone can really be happy because one person's happiness often leads to someone else's unhappiness. Rising divorce rates, declining marriage rates, increasing drug use, acceptance of homosexuality, demands that the public accept gender changes and open public restrooms to individuals of the opposite biological sex, increasing crime rates, and decrease of discipline in the public schools, are the result of individual demands that they be happy. Individual happiness is worshiped in our society and adverse secondary effects are ignored.

In the time of Jesus and Paul, there was another group dedicated to pursuing happiness as their ultimate goal. These were the Epicureans. They had sense enough to realize that while happiness was the ultimate goal, sometimes some happiness had to be sacrificed now, so that more happiness could be attained later. Therefore, while eating a croissant taken from a store without paying for it might make them immediately happy, they understood that if such an action led to arrest for shoplifting and subsequent imprisonment, the amount of happiness attained later in life during the course of the imprisonment would be far less than if they were free. Therefore they should abstain from shoplifting the croissant to maximize their lifelong happiness!

There was no absolute right and wrong, but there was the concept of consequentialism. In other words, what are the likely consequences? What is the chance the consequences will happen? This would be weighed against the perceived benefit of doing the action, i.e. stealing is not prohibited, in their philosophy, if you most likely would get away with it, and if caught, the consequences would be light. While many of us may not identify ourselves as Epicureans, we definitely do take a cost-benefit approach to our morality more often than we would like to admit.

Jesus also talked about happiness in the opening words of His Sermon on the Mount. He definitely took the *indirect* approach to achieving happiness. In each of His eight Beatitudes, Jesus describes the type of person who is blessed or happy. At first glance, the attributes Jesus describes seem opposite to what we think is required to be happy. But Jesus takes the very long-term approach. He looks at the ultimate cost-benefits. After all, *"For what shall it profit a man, if he shall gain the whole world, and lose his own soul?"* Mark 8:36.

He begins with the proposition that there is a God, and that God rewards the righteous and punishes the wicked. The ultimate reward of the righteous, of course, is being granted status as a child of God in the Kingdom of God. This status leads to eternal happiness, which far exceeds any temporal happiness sacrificed in achieving this goal.

I will argue in this book that Jesus does not tell us how to get saved in His Beatitudes (He does that elsewhere in the Bible) instead He describes what saved people look like. Furthermore, saved people are happy people. They are blessed in this life as well as the next.

In the Gospels, Jesus spends a lot more time telling us how to live happily as Kingdom people than He does trying to convince us to join up as new believers. This book entitled, *Keys to a Happy Life: The Beatitudes According to Jesus* delves into the teachings of Jesus on what it takes to be happy. When we are saved, we are saved into eternal life, and that life begins today; not after we die. As Kingdom people, we have been saved into a walk with Christ, and into a lifestyle that is compelling, powerful, and different than the world around us.

The Beatitudes are a beautiful and poetic introduction to the Sermon on the Mount. Some have felt they paint a picture of perfection that we can never achieve until the next life. Others have said that they were meant to confound us, so that we would know we need grace. Still others have felt they are the essence of the gospel and a road map of how we can work our way to salvation. I believe that they are simply a picture of the characteristics and attributes of people who are already saved. *The Beatitudes show us the fruit of salvation, not the road map to it.* Elsewhere, scripture is clear that we are saved by God's grace, through faith in His Son Jesus Christ. Jesus said, "You will know them by their fruit." People who are saved will bear good fruit.

To be truly happy in this life, we must be true to that inner Spirit of Christ which we received at the moment of our salvation. Jesus shows us in His Beatitudes and in His other teachings, what we must do to live truly happy and fruitful lives. Often, the path Jesus paints to happiness and fulfillment is contrary to the way our flesh and natural mind want to lead us. The path of Jesus does not go straight from point A to point B, but often takes surprising and unexpected turns!

A SOMEWHAT SCHOLARLY NOTE

In the course of this book, we are going to take a devotional look at each of Jesus' eight beatitudes recorded in the Book of Matthew. I say this is a devotional look because this is not a scholarly document. If this were a scholarly look at the Beatitudes, it would have surveyed 40 or 50 works written by other scholars, both Jewish and Christian, on the meanings and tenses of words, delving into whether such words were even written by Matthew or spoken by the Lord, and after exhaustive treatment of the subject, with copious footnotes to be sure, it would have made little difference in the reader's life.

This is a devotional work. I say *devotional*, because my primary intent is for you, the reader, to take a closer look at familiar passages in the Bible, and to reflect upon them in a way which might affect your life. The Beatitudes are short little poetic quips of Jesus, which are often memorized but seldom reflected upon! As you reflect on these quips, see if the Holy Spirit might just quicken something in your spirit and motivate you to examine something in your Christian walk.

Before we launch into our devotional look at the Beatitudes, I do wish to touch on a few things that you might consider somewhat scholarly just to give you some interesting background that might help as you consider the Beatitudes of our Lord. If the following paragraphs are too scholarly for your taste, just skip over them and launch into the first chapter and enjoy.

A Jewish friend asked me, "What are the Beatitudes, and why do they call them that?" Both Matthew and Luke record some of Jesus' Beatitudes. Matthew records eight of them, Luke records four. The four recorded by Luke are *similar to* but slightly different than the eight recorded in Matthew. This book concentrates on the eight Beatitudes recorded in Matthew. Using the New International Version (NIV) Bible translation, the eight Beatitudes of Jesus recorded by Matthew in Matt. 5:3-10 are as follow:

> ***Blessed are the poor in spirit,***
> ***for theirs is the kingdom of heaven.***
> ***Blessed are those who mourn,***
> ***for they will be comforted.***
> ***Blessed are the meek,***
> ***for they will inherit the earth.***
> ***Blessed are those who hunger and thirst for***
> ***righteousness, for they will be filled.***
> ***Blessed are the merciful,***
> ***for they will be shown mercy.***
> ***Blessed are the pure in heart,***
> ***for they will see God.***
> ***Blessed are the peacemakers,***
> ***for they will be called sons of God.***
> ***Blessed are those who are persecuted because of***
> ***righteousness, for theirs is the kingdom of heaven.***

Following this last Beatitude, Jesus launches into some teaching applying the meaning of this last Beatitude to His disciples. He states, "Blessed are you when people insult you, persecute you and falsely say all kinds of evil against you because of me. Rejoice and be glad, because great is your reward in heaven, for in the same way they persecuted the prophets who were before you." Matt. 5:11-12 (NIV).

If you look at each of these eight Beatitudes, you will see that they begin with the words, *Blessed are.* During the time that much of our English theological terminology was formed, the Roman Catholic Church ruled the theological landscape, and it used the Latin Vulgate translation of the Bible. The Roman Catholic scholars wrote their dissertations in Latin. If you were to examine the Latin Vulgate translation of these verses, you would see that they all begin with the phrase, *Beati* which comes from the Latin word *beatitudo* which means "Happy, fortunate or blissful." From this we derive the English word, *Beatitudes.* Speaking of the Vulgate version, in the Latin Bible the order of the second and third Beatitudes are reversed, lumping poor in spirit and meek together. Some Catholic translations of the Bible keep this Latin order. In this book, we follow the order of the Greek Bible which predates the Latin version.

Before we examine, just what it means to *be blessed,* we should understand just a few more linguistic points. The book of Matthew was originally written in Greek, but when Jesus was speaking, He was not speaking in Greek. Instead, likely he was speaking in Aramaic, and quoting concepts from what we call, the Old Testament, which was written in Hebrew. As scholars do their scholarly work, they try to look at the linguistic background of the words written, the words spoken, and the source of the quotations derived in order to come up with possible nuances and understandings. We will not delve so deeply because it is unlikely that Jesus' hearers would have understood all that anyway. At the same time, His hearers may have had some background in the Jewish Scripture that would be lost on the average 21st Century Christian reader, and where relevant, I will try to fill in some of that background in the course of this book.

Sparing you the blow by blow linguistic study of the word used by Jesus at the beginning of each Beatitude, we see that in the Greek, the word used means *fortunate*, or *happy*. The Hebrew word which Jesus likely spoke or referred to in OT Scripture is *Ashre* which derives from the verb *Ashar* which means *happy*, or *blessed*. Later Hebrew scholars also attach the nuance *praiseworthy* to the word. All of these meanings intersect to paint a picture for the word to mean *happy, praiseworthy, fortunate,* and/or *blessed*. Such a person is living exactly where he or she should be. Who would not want to exist on such a plane of being?

CHAPTER 1

THE FOUNDATION OF SAVING FAITH

Blessed are the poor in spirit
for theirs is the Kingdom of Heaven
Matt. 5:3

These days, humility is not a much sought after virtue. Neither is poverty. Coast through the internet, and we are constantly being reminded to "stand tall," "be proud," "don't let others walk on you," "get what is yours." In our culture *pride* is a key virtue. People are even proud of their sins, and the rest of us are reminded, if we don't like it, we can go pound sand…Jesus taught us other things.

According to Matthew, following His Temptation and choosing of His disciples, He began His ministry with the Sermon on the Mount, and He began this with the Beatitudes. Matthew has eight Beatitudes. We will spend some time in this book, exploring these Beatitudes one by one. The first one is *Blessed are the poor in spirit, for theirs is the Kingdom of Heaven.* In the Gospel of Luke, Chapter 6, he records only four, and the wording of the first is slightly different, it reads *Blessed are you who are poor, for yours is the Kingdom of God.*

In each of the Beatitudes, Matthew's and Luke's, the verse begins with the word *blessed*. It then sets forth a quality or characteristic of the person being described, and finally states a reward that such a person will receive. In this Beatitude, Jesus says that people who are poor in spirit will be *blessed* because they are going to receive the kingdom of heaven. Since all of us want to go to heaven when we die, we must immediately pay great attention to this Beatitude. But many questions immediately come to mind. The initial question that must be answered is, *How do the Beatitudes square with the rest of the gospel?*

The reason I ask the above question is because on the face of it, sometimes, what Jesus teaches about salvation does not match up exactly with what Paul seems to teach. For instance, the essence of Pauline teaching is that we are saved by grace, through faith, alone. He does not mention being poor in spirit. There will be other issues that come up between Jesus and Paul, if we read the Scripture on a superficial level. So the initial question which we must deal with is....

ARE THE BEATITUDES MEANT FOR MODERN DAY CHRISTIANS?

In some Protestant Churches, which follow an extreme brand of dispensationalism, pastors have found much of the teachings of Jesus as problematic and tried to write them off as belonging to a prior dispensation. They treat these red letter teachings of Christ much like the rest of Christendom views the Jewish ceremonial and food laws. They say that just as the Jewish food laws do not apply to Christians after the resurrection of Christ, neither do the teachings of Jesus on the Sermon on the Mount apply to us modern believers. According to them, Jesus was only teaching the Jews who would hear Him prior to the Resurrection. They do this because they feel that the teachings of Jesus conflict with what they understand to be Paul's gospel of grace. Seizing on some of Paul's teachings, they emphasize that salvation comes only from faith, which does not even ultimately come from us, and that there is nothing we can do to add to or contribute to our salvation. Jesus on the other hand teaches about all kinds of things that His followers need to do and be in order to be saved. This creates an apparent conflict, so these teachers assign the teachings of Christ to the Jews during the life of Christ only. They hold Christ's teachings are no longer relevant for Christians once Jesus rose from the dead.

I reject this view in the strongest terms. The Gospels were not written until some decades after the death and resurrection of Christ. Are we to say that they are filled with irrelevant teachings, no longer applicable as soon as the ink dried on the paper? Did Jesus merely come to die? Was His ministry a waste of time? Why fill his disciples with teachings for three years, if they were only meant to forget them upon His resurrection?

No. If these pastors find the teachings of Christ irreconcilable with the teachings of Paul as they understand it, then perhaps they need to readjust their understanding of Paul to accommodate the teaching of the incarnate God! Rather than trying to jettison the teachings of God in the flesh, they need to account for it in their understanding of Paul's true teachings.

I say we must try to understand Jesus on His own terms, reconciling His teachings with those of Paul, so that we can hear the message of the **whole** New Testament in balance.

The problem with Jesus, according to some of these teachers, is that when we read Jesus' teachings, He seems to interject other things into our salvation other than faith alone. He seems to indicate that how you live your life, the attitudes you hold, the choices you make and the things you do as a believer are also important to your ultimate destiny. We must be very careful, indeed, if we find ourselves so attached to a particular theological doctrine written by man, that we feel we must discount the words of the Son of God in order to make our system work!

We **can** read Jesus in such a way as to avoid setting up irreconcilable conflicts between Jesus and Paul. This should always be our first choice in reading Jesus as well as reading Paul. We should read them so they complement one another rather than conflict. Does that make sense?

Using this way of interpretation and applying it to the Beatitudes, we can understand that Jesus is not telling us about what we *must do to be saved* but rather he is describing *what we do when we are saved.* In other words, *what do saved people look like?* Some preachers refer to the Beatitudes as *BE ATTITUDES.* Paul talks all about what we must believe to be saved. Jesus teaches us what saved people look like, how saved people act, and what kind of attitudes saved people have. He invites us to look at our own lives and compare. If we do not look like this, act like this, or have these types of attitudes, then we are right to question whether or not we really have saving faith!

GO AND MAKE DISCIPLES...

In the Great Commission, Jesus calls us to go forth "and make disciples in all Nations, baptizing them in the Name of the Father, the Son, and the Holy Spirit, and teaching them to obey everything I have commanded." Matt. 28:19-20. He doesn't call on the Apostles to go forth and get people to assent to a certain set of facts and say the sinner's prayer only. He calls on them to go forth and make disciples, and to teach disciples to obey. Jesus teaches us what it means to be His disciple. I would add that Jesus made this command AFTER His resurrection. He didn't say, "Hey guys, all that stuff I taught you before now...it is irrelevant. It only applied to you during the three years of my ministry, but not now." Rather, He stated that we must teach His disciples to *obey* Him, not *ignore* Him!

Having a firm conviction, then, that the Beatitudes DO APPLY TO US, let us see if we can understand and apply them without doing too much violence to our understanding of the rest of the Bible!

WHAT DOES IT MEAN TO BE BLESSED?

Every verse begins with the word *blessed.* Some modern translations use the word *happy.* The Greek for this word is *makarioi.* It means more than just being happy.

Happiness is an emotional reaction to favorable circumstances that happen to an individual. It is changeable depending on outside events and how we react to them. One day you are happy, the next you are sad.

Blessedness is a state of being. It is the existence of an individual who has received something from God. What we receive from God is grace. Something we did not earn, but it comes to us when we place our faith in Christ. It is the condition of being touched by the grace of God which MAY lead to emotions of joy or happiness, but is also with us, even when we are temporarily sad.

After the initial description of *blessed* in each Beatitude, come the description of a person, and the reward they are to expect. In the first Beatitude the reward is attainment of the *Kingdom of Heaven* or the *Kingdom of God.* These two are interchangeable.

THE KINGDOM OF HEAVEN

Obviously, the Kingdom of Heaven is what we are all shooting for. We want eternal life with God, however that may look, especially when we consider the alternative.

Michael L. Faber

When we trust in Christ as our Savior and when the Holy Spirit resides in us, we have become members of God's forever family, and eternal life is ours. One thing to understand, Jesus says, *theirs IS the Kingdom of Heaven* not *they will go to heaven when they die.* In my prior book <u>Meditations on the Lord's Prayer</u>, I discussed the concept of the Kingdom of God in the chapter dealing with Christ's words, *Thy Kingdom come, Thy will be done, on earth as it is in heaven.* Obtaining the Kingdom of Heaven is attaining *eternal* life by becoming adopted into God's forever family. Eternal life is eternal: past, present and future. It begins now, not someday. When we are saved, we begin living out our eternity with God, *right now.*

In other words, the goal of every Christian is to obtain the Kingdom of Heaven or the Kingdom of God. This implies both a soteriological component and an eschatological component. These are big words meaning that we receive citizenship in the Kingdom of Heaven when we are saved, and as part and parcel of our salvation. We begin *establishing* the Kingdom of Heaven in our hearts and in the world around us, right now! The Kingdom of Heaven is wherever God's people are performing God's will. We are beginning a task that Christ will complete when He comes again. People who are members of the Kingdom of Heaven are poor in spirit.

WHAT TYPE OF PEOPLE ARE BLESSED WITH THE KINGDOM OF HEAVEN?

The middle part of the Beatitude describes what type of people attain the reward described at the end of the Beatitude. In this case, Matthew says, *Blessed are the poor in spirit*, while Luke says only *Blessed are you Poor*.

Let's look at Luke's version first.

DOES ECONOMIC STATUS REALLY DETERMINE OUR SALVATION?

In this world, the rich and the poor often struggle against one another. The rich often oppress the poor to gain their riches, and the poor often struggle against the rich to pull them down. The rich see the poor as lazy and shiftless, and the poor see the rich as greedy, out of touch and heartless. We have seen this struggle in Marxism, and we see it in President Obama's speeches as he pits the 98% against the 2% to gain political advantage. In human history, this struggle goes on and on. Sometimes the poor are successful in pulling down the rich, but the leaders of the poor become the new rich, and everything starts all over again. Many of you have seen this in countries and companies around the world. Nothing new is under the sun.

Does Jesus take sides? Is He teaching that those who are economically successful will go to hell, while those who are downtrodden are automatically saved? Reading the scripture literally, this would seem to be the case. If so, what is the economic dividing line for rich versus poor? Should we look to the whole world, in which case *everyone in America* is probably doomed since even our poor are rich when compared to starving people in Africa and Asia? Should we only compare to those of our own town, so that those on the bottom are secure in salvation, but not those at the top? If so, who is doomed? The top 2%, 10%, 20%?

How about the wicked poor? Those poor who are drug dealers, pimps, murderers, child molesters and gang bangers? Are they going to heaven because they are too lazy to get a job and choose to subsist on public assistance? No, something is wrong with this picture. It does not fit with the rest of the Bible, and the rest of Jesus' teachings. This leads us to something we must understand. While you can just pick up the Bible and read it, you may often read it wrong.

INTERPRETING SCRIPTURE

If we want to read scripture with a correct understanding, we need to "study ....rightly dividing the word of truth." 2 Tim. 2:15. People studying the Bible have set up some general principles to use when studying the Scripture. These principles are not sacrosanct, but they are helpful. What are they?

Scripture should not always be read literally, it should be interpreted against itself.

Don't just read one verse and build a theology out of it.

If the verse doesn't match with the message of the whole Bible, it must be interpreted in such a way that we keep the meanings of the words while maintaining the integrity of the whole scripture.

Remember, all scripture is inspired and useful for teaching, rebuking, correcting, and training in righteousness.

Also, we should remember that Jesus also often uses hyperbole in His teaching.

Hyperbole is an extreme statement that is not meant to be taken literally, but it is said for effect to make a point.

An example of hyperbole is when Jesus says, *if your right eye causes you to stumble, gouge it out and throw it away!* Matt. 5:29. He was making a statement about the necessity of avoiding things that make you stumble and sin, He was not telling you to actually remove your eyeball. But we must **interpret** Jesus' literal words to come to this conclusion.

HOW HAVE OTHERS INTERPRETED THIS PASSAGE ABOUT THE POOR RECEIVING THE KINGDOM OF GOD?

The Catholic Church has used this verse in conjunction with others to conclude that God has a preference for the poor. Not that the poor are automatically saved. God's supposed "preference for the poor" may be true to a degree because in the whole Bible, God does seem to come to the rescue of the underdog quite often. He reminds the Jews in the Law of Moses to remember now that they are in power that they were once strangers. He directs them to take special care for the widow, the orphans, and the strangers who are economically and politically vulnerable. God does not hate the rich or deny us (those in the Western world) salvation just because we have material assets, but He does have a special heart for the poor and the oppressed. This is true whether the poor are Jews, African slaves, or any other group of people on the receiving end of systematic mistreatment. *God hears the cry of the poor.*

WHAT ABOUT "BLESSED ARE THE POOR"?

We have seen above that even without considering Paul, it does not make sense to read this literally. We must interpret it, especially in light of the fact that Paul teaches quite clearly that salvation comes through faith in Christ, by the grace of God.

Let me ask you… Where are there more churches? Rich neighborhoods or poor? Who occupies our churches more? Rich or poor? Educated or uneducated? Who prays more? Those whose physical needs are satisfied, or those who are in want and in danger?

If salvation comes by faith alone in Jesus Christ by the grace of God, **who is more likely to believe and accept this?** The rich or the poor? The educated or the uneducated?

I have a friend in India, Pastor Gabriel Muppidi, who is ministering among the poorest of the poor. He refers to his flock as "scavenger people." They are people, who because of their caste, must dig around in garbage dumps for things to eat, and things to sell so they can have money to eat. They have little education and little economic hope. They are poor. But they are receiving the gospel in droves. He regularly sends me pictures of new people being baptized and receiving the Lord! Praise God! But I guarantee you, he would not be so successful if he were preaching to the Hindu upper castes. His flock are people at the bottom who need help, and they know they need help. They are ready to receive the Gospel.

Read in light of the whole gospel, and the whole Bible, we can see Jesus is simply stating a fact when he calls the poor *blessed,* **because they are receiving the Kingdom of Heaven.**

Paul himself wrote, "Brothers, think of what you were when you were called. Not many of you were wise by human standards; not many were influential; not many were of noble birth. But God chose the foolish things of the world to shame the wise; God chose the weak things of the world to shame the strong." I Cor. 1:26-27.

Jesus describes a situation. The poor are *blessed* because they are more likely to accept the Gospel. And when they do, theirs will be the Kingdom of God. This doesn't mean that the rich won't be saved. It just means that if you are poor, you are more likely to believe, and more likely to receive the blessing of eternal life than those who are well off now.

Matthew refines the conflict even more by his wording *Blessed are the poor in spirit.*

WHAT DOES IT MEAN TO BE POOR IN SPIRIT?

The words, "poor in spirit" occur only once in the Bible, right here. But everyone agrees that being "poor in spirit" is to be humble. Proverbs 16:19 has a similar verse which says, "Better to be humble in spirit with the lowly, than to divide the spoil with the proud."

The poor man knows he is lacking in resources.

He knows he needs help to get by.

The extremely poor know that they will die if they don't receive assistance.

Someone who is *poor in spirit* knows he lacks sufficient spiritual resources to attain eternal life on his own. He is aware of his sin and his weakness.

A great example of this was taught by Jesus Himself in the Parable of Tax Collector and the Pharisee (Luke 18:10-14).

Remember the Parable of the Tax Collector and the Pharisee? I don't believe this parable has the power today that it did at the time. Today, when we hear the word *Pharisee* we think of hypocrites who opposed Jesus, and thus we think ill of them. But at that time, they were the best of the best when it came to faith in God. They attended church regularly; they obeyed the law of God assiduously; they gave generously. On the other hand, while we may not like paying our taxes, we don't look down on employees of the IRS or the Franchise Tax Board in the same way that First Century Jews did on their tax collectors. Back then, tax collectors were considered traitors to their people, and they were often immoral and corrupt as well. I would like to update this parable now, so you can get the power of it.

One day, at Faith Presbyterian Church, two men walked into the chapel at lunch time for some prayer. The first man was an Evangelical Pastor. He began his prayer, "Thank you Lord that I am your child. Thank you that I don't smoke, gamble, drink alcohol, or look at pornography. I am proud to tithe 10% of my net earnings to my local church body and to attend church every Sunday…unlike that guy next to me who doesn't even look as if he belongs here. Amen." Then he left.

The second man was a drug abusing porn star. All decked out in a silk shirt and tight pants with a gold necklace. He fell to the floor weeping, "I've just been diagnosed with AIDS. I know what I have been doing is wrong. I know I don't even belong here! But please forgive me. I am a sinner. I don't know what else to do." With tears in his eyes, he got up and left.

Irrespective of whether the pastor was "saved," which of these two men met God that day? Which did not?

Which was poor in spirit? Which not?

Humility is the key to entering the Kingdom. Jesus said you must be like the little children. Why? They are humble in comparison to adults. They are not afraid to admit their need for care, love, and protection.

When you are proud, you will not admit that you need ANYTHING from ANYONE, including God. You have everything worked out. You are self-sufficient. You don't need to change anything. It is all taken care of.

When you are proud of yourself, including your sins, you see your failings as strengths. If this is your attitude, you have no need to repent. In my humble opinion, this is the **deadly ingredient** of the modern gay movement. It is not that the sin of homosexual sex is any worse than other varieties of fornication, or lust, greed, gossip, etc. BUT, all the rest of us know we are sinners, and are aware of our sins and know we need to repent. We know that we fail to live up to God's standards when we sin. But the young people in the gay movement are taught to be proud of their sin, and to even deny it is a sin. They are taught, through shared websites, to either twist the Scripture to teach what is does not, or even worse, to deny God's standards, and to denounce a God that opposes what they do as unloving, and thus not worthy of worship. They are in rebellion against God. I fear for them.

With pride....*there is no need to repent.*

I do not wish to pick on homosexuals alone with this condemnation of pride. We can pick on rich successful people as well. They have worked themselves up from the bottom. Made all the "right decisions," and accumulated vast wealth. They are proud of their success, and proud of their greed. They see no need to repent. I live in an affluent neighborhood, and I can tell you, I see precious few of my neighbors leaving for church, any given Sunday. They are busy riding their bicycles, rafting, golfing or watching their big screen TV's. They don't need God-they think-because they have everything they want.

If you are self-sufficient, i.e., lacking in poverty…you may think you have no need for a Savior.

The Bible says, *God opposes the proud, but gives grace to the humble.* James 4:6. Meditate on this for a second. God opposes the proud. Instead, He gives grace to the humble. Grace is what we need for salvation! Without grace we are doomed. As Paul explains, "We are saved by grace, through faith… and not by works lest any man should boast." Ephesians 2:8-9. **Again we see boasting and pride as the enemy of salvation.**

John W. Miller in his book The Christian Way wrote, "Humility or poverty of spirit is not a matter of thinking low thoughts about ourselves. It is not a matter of groveling in the dust. It is simply a matter of knowing ourselves as we truly are. And when we see ourselves as we really are, we will see that we are poor."

People who have poverty of economics, and even more so, poverty of spirit, have fewer barriers to that repentance before God which is necessary for the receiving of saving Grace.

CONCLUSION

Jesse Ventura, the big-time wrestler who became Governor of Minnesota, declared, *Christianity is a crutch.* I say, *Amen to that, Brother! A crutch is a great thing to have when you are crippled!*

We are all crippled. We cannot make the journey on our own. We can only achieve salvation by the grace of God, and He gives it to us when we are willing to repent of our sins and place our faith in Christ. We will not do this if we are proud and self-sufficient.

Instead, let us be humble, let us be poor in spirit, for indeed, *Blessed are the poor in spirit, for theirs is the Kingdom of God.* Being humble, being poor in spirit is the *foundation of saving faith*!

Will you put aside your pride today, and accept Jesus Christ as your Lord and Savior? Joining God's forever family through saving faith in Jesus Christ is the first step to a truly happy and blessed life…eternal life.

REFLECTIONS:
1. What is the best thing to do when we come upon two scriptures that are seemingly contradictory?
2. Paul says we need faith in Christ for salvation. Jesus says the poor in spirit shall receive the Kingdom of Heaven. How can we reconcile these two seemingly contradictory scriptures?
3. Why are poor people blessed? Isn't wealth a sign of God's blessing?

4. Why do poor people often attend church in greater numbers than the wealthy?
5. How is "Christianity a crutch"? Is that a good thing or a bad thing?
6. What is the difference between being blessed and being happy?
7. Can blessed people be unhappy? Can happy people be un-blessed?
8. In what ways does God oppose the proud?
9. What is the essential ingredient for saving faith?

CHAPTER 2

SHARING THE HEART OF GOD

Blessed are those who mourn,
for they shall be comforted
Matt. 5:4

These days, everyone wants to be happy. It is our right. Doesn't the Declaration of Independence say that every man has the right to *life, liberty and the pursuit of happiness?* Part of what we expect out of our Christian faith is joy. There is certainly a place in our faith, a big place, for being happy and joyful. But Jesus reveals to us that there is also a time to mourn. In fact, during His Sermon on the Mount, Jesus declared, *Blessed are those who mourn, for they shall be comforted.* Matt. 5:4. Why does Jesus place such an emphasis on mourning? Why would He say that those who mourn will be blessed by comfort? Like all of the Beatitudes, this one must be interpreted in the light of other Scripture and the message of the whole Bible.

CLEAR ALLUSION TO THE COMING OF THE MESSIAH

Living in a modern Western Christian society, it is easy to approach such a simple verse and read into it a meaning that is entirely unrelated to how it was intended, and how it was heard. I have heard it taught that this Beatitude means something like, *When our loved ones die, we should take comfort in the fact that we will see them again someday in heaven.* That's nice. It might be true IF our loved ones were Christians, and IF we ourselves are true Christians, but this is not what was intended, nor what was heard by the people who attended the Sermon on the Mount. To understand the full impact of this sentence, we need to understand the *context* in which it was spoken.

First of all, these words were initially spoken to Jews who were immersed in the Old Testament prophecies, and who were eagerly awaiting a Messiah to deliver them from Roman oppression. The Jews were no strangers to mourning. What they mourned was not a loss of their loved ones whom they hoped to see again in heaven one day. What they mourned was the loss of their land and the loss of their freedom which occurred as a result of the judgment of God for the sins of their land, and their people. They were well aware of the fact that their nation had broken its covenant with God, and God had in turn punished them by allowing foreign peoples to conquer them.

The Jewish people mourned their sin, and its consequences, and the comfort they hoped for was the restoration of their freedom and the restoration of their land. They were looking forward to the Great Deliverer!

Just before Jesus preached the Sermon on the Mount and before He chose the Twelve Apostles, He launched His ministry in Nazareth by reading from Isaiah Chapter 61 and declared, *Today, this scripture is fulfilled in your hearing.* Luke 4:16-21. While the snippet of this passage recorded by Luke does not apparently refer to mourning or to comfort, if we turn the pages of our Bibles to Isaiah 61:1-3, we will see the rest of the story. In verse 1, the speaker, whom the Spirit has anointed, has come to *bind up the broken hearted.* In verse 2, he is to *comfort all those who mourn*, and in verse 3 he will *bestow on them a crown of beauty instead of ashes, the oil of gladness instead of mourning and a garment of praise instead of a spirit of despair.* All of these verses make it clear that the Messiah will be comforting those who mourn. This is what the Jews were waiting for, and in His Sermon on the Mount, Jesus declares, *Blessed are those who mourn, for they shall be comforted.* The meaning of this Beatitude is clear. It is a statement of Messianic fulfillment. The time for comfort spoken of by the Prophet Isaiah has come. The Messiah is here!

MOURNING IS DESCRIPTIVE OF THE CHILDREN OF GOD WHO SHARE HIS HEART

In the last chapter, I set out the idea that the Beatitudes are a description of the followers of Christ. Apart from the Messianic prophetic undertones of this Beatitude as described above, how does it describe a Christ-follower today? Why should we, who follow Christ, mourn? And if we do mourn, why will we be blessed?

I will set out below three reasons why true followers of Christ mourn. In preview, they are: 1) we are mourning the sins of society that set us apart from the sin of the land; 2) our mourning leads to repentance of personal sin; and 3) mourning motivates us to evangelize, pray for others, and act to lessen the impact of sin around us.

Before I touch on these three reasons for mourning, let me first say that mourning allows us to share the heart of God.

As we grow in our walk with Christ, we begin to see things more and more through the eyes of Jesus. Since Jesus is part of the Godhead, this means that as we walk with Christ, we begin to see things more and more through the eyes of God. This is because as we allow the Holy Spirit to lead us, He begins to transform our minds allowing us to see things accurately as God does! Cf. Rom. 12:2.

Did you know that God mourns? He sees the world that He created, and He knows what we are capable of becoming, and yet we continually choose lesser and darker paths in our misguided attempts to secure immediate happiness. As we make these lesser choices we harm ourselves and harm those around us. For this God grieves.

My mother, Elaine Faber, wrote a short story called *Kitten, Kitten* based on a real-life event. I will summarize it. You see, she is a cat-lover. When I was a kid, we often had more than 10 cats, as my mother was a cat lover. She raised Persian cats. One day while at work, she noticed a fat, female, feral cat. Having been a cat-breeder, she knew what this meant. This feral cat was nasty and mangled, and before her pregnancy, thin with ribs showing, and stickers on her fur. My mother decided she was going to rescue the kittens after they were born and give them a good home, so she kept an eye on this cat. The cat disappeared for a few months. Then one day my mother spotted the feral cat with its three feral kittens. By this time, these kittens looked like their mother. Stickers in their fur, fleas on their body, and infections in their eyes.

For those of you who don't know, a feral cat is a wild cat, one which has not been raised by people. Feral cats are mean and nasty, and likely to scratch and bite you if you attempt to pick one up. They think you want to hurt them. Knowing this, my mother grabbed a box which she was keeping in her car for the occasion. She attempted to pick up the kittens. They scratched, bit and ran, doing everything they could to avoid getting caught by this intruding human. They even ran into the bushes with my mother behind them. Despite the kitten scratches and bites, and the bush stickers, she managed to catch one and put it in her box. As she went after the second kitten, the first was doing its best to climb out of the box. She caught the second kitten, and while both were trying to escape the box, she chased the third. The third kitten was too fast, too smart, and too mean to get caught, and eventually she abandoned the effort and went home with the two.

Months later, the two kittens were as happy as could be. Their fleas were removed, their eye infections were treated, they had their shots, their fur was clean and knot-free, their bellies were full, and they enjoyed the love and affection they received from my mother as they played with their new toys. Even though my mother was very happy with the company of these two precious kittens, she always had an empty spot in her heart for the one that got away.

We are like these kittens. God wants to give us the good life, to feed us, love us, and provide us protection, but we see Him as a threat, and we struggle, claw, and fight to maintain our freedom to be sick, hungry, and infected. He manages to snatch some of us, but even then, we are doing our best to climb out of the box, as we are tempted by the allure of sin. Finally, even when God has rescued some of us, His heart still aches for those who got away, and continue to live in their broken lifestyles.

WHY DO WE MOURN?

When I told my friend, Paul, I was going to preach on *Blessed are those who mourn,* he piped up and asked, *Are you using Ezekiel chapters 8 and 9?* Embarrassed, I responded, *Well, I might if I knew what it was!* We looked it up together. These chapters recount a vision of the prophet Ezekiel, while he was an exile in Babylon. At this time in history, Judah was on the way down. Babylon would later destroy the entire country and carry off the people into exile and slavery for 75 years, but this hadn't happened yet. Only some of the elite, like Ezekiel, had been taken hostage to Babylon, while Jewish kings still reigned in Jerusalem. In his vision, the Holy Spirit picked

Ezekiel up by his hair, and transported him miraculously from Babylon to the Jerusalem Temple 500 miles away. God then showed Ezekiel the secret idolatry going on in the temple as well as the violence in society. This enraged God, and He swore to take His protection and presence away from the Temple and to destroy the city. He brought six angelic destroyers and an angelic scribe before Ezekiel and instructed the destroyers to kill everyone in the city. However, He asked the scribe to go first throughout the city and "put a mark on the foreheads of those who grieve and lament over all the detestable things that are done in it." Ezekiel 9:4. God then told the destroyers to spare those with the mark, and destroy the rest. This was a vision, and didn't actually happen, though soon after the whole city was destroyed.

THE FIRST REASON WE MOURN IS TO SEPARATE OURSELVES FROM BEING IDENTIFIED WITH THE SIN HAPPENING ALL AROUND US

Ezekiel's vision makes a point. Even though sometimes it seems as if the whole world is going bad, there are always those who do not agree, and who should not be held responsible. Frankly, I believe our Western society is quickly going down the toilet. I also believe that if *every* Christian stood up and spoke against what is going on, and voted against what is going on, we could stop the decline, or slow it down significantly. But we don't! We cover our eyes, we cover our ears, and we cover our mouths, saying, *It is not our business.* Imagine a woman being raped by a punk on a public bus full of 20 other full-grown men. The punk does the raping, 3 or 4 other of the passengers cheer the punk on, and the other 16 men look the other way and pretend not to notice. Yes, the punk is criminally liable. The cheering onlookers are also criminally liable as aiders and abettors. While the other 16 may not be criminally liable, they are **morally** responsible for not stepping in and stopping the atrocity! We are those 16 men, when we do not actively *mourn* the sinfulness so flagrantly being practiced in our society. While we may not be criminally responsible, God makes it clear in His revelation to Ezekiel that we will still be accountable, unless we do something to separate ourselves from this sin. One of the ways to do this is by mourning and lamenting.

THE SECOND REASON WE MOURN IS TO TRULY REPENT OF OUR OWN PERSONAL SIN

The Bible says, *Godly sorrow brings repentance that leads to salvation and leaves no regret, but worldly sorrow brings death.* 2 Cor. 7:10. Godly sorrow is another way of saying mourning. We all sin, and we have all fallen short of the glory of God. But we are not just to accept this fact and say, *Praise God! Jesus paid it all.* And then move on in our lives continuing to sin. No. The first words of preaching spoken by Jesus to the people at the beginning of His ministry were, *Repent, for the Kingdom of Heaven is near.* Matt. 4:17. Godly sorrow brings repentance. It is repentance that leads to salvation. Our sin brings not only spiritual death to those who never are saved, but it brings physical death to those, Christian or not, who continue in their sin, and it brings harm to ourselves and our loved ones. Sin grieves God, and destroys our witness. While we will never entirely eliminate sin from our lives, we are always called upon by God to confess it, to struggle against it, and to participate in the process of sanctification, which means growing more and more away from sin as we progress in our spiritual lives.

To repent means to turn from and go the opposite way. While we are practicing sin, we are walking in the way of Satan away from God. When we repent, we turn from Satan and his ways, and begin walking back towards God. Salvation, according to 2 Cor. 7:10, requires repentance, and repentance requires godly sorrow. Sin is attractive and alluring to our flesh. That is why we practice it. *Only by seeing our actions from God's perspective, and seeing the harm caused by sin, can we truly repent from it, and leave it behind. This requires prayer.*

God doesn't want us just to mouth an insincere apology so we can be forgiven. He truly wants us to walk powerful, Spirit-filled, and sin-free lives. He wants us to turn our backs on sin and walk toward Him, and with Him, to the life that He has intended for us. The only way this can be accomplished is through true repentance. The only way this can be accomplished is through *godly sorrow*.

As you pray, ask the Holy Spirit to reveal to you the sin in your lives. He will be happy to shine that Holy

Ghost spotlight on every aspect of your life where you are falling short. Then ask Him to show you how these sins affect your life and those around you. He will reveal the harm of these actions. Ask Him for His heart in these matters, and He will allow you to experience the grief that He feels as the result of your wrong choices. As you feel this grief, embrace it, and allow it to motivate you to truly break away from the grip which this sin has on your life! This process may need to be repeated, because the truth is, we really like to sin. Sin temporarily makes us happy, and that is why we do it. But in the end, it is a delicious-tasting, slow-acting poison! While it temporarily quenches our thirst, it is killing us from the inside as well as those we touch. Feel the grief of God towards this sin, and allow Him to give you the strength to repent!

THE THIRD REASON WE MOURN FOR THE SINS OF SOCIETY IS TO MOTIVATE US TO EVANGELIZE, TO PRAY FOR OTHERS, AND TO ACT TO MITIGATE THE ILL-EFFECTS OF SIN

Not only do we mourn for our own sin, but we also mourn the sins of our society, so we can react correctly. Earlier, I stated that everybody wants to be happy. Each one of us is lonely, and hurting, and needy in some way. Each one of us deserves some kind of happiness, but due to our sin-nature, we look for happiness in all the wrong places. Not only are we confused, but society as a whole is confused. Look at the things we are doing and promoting as a culture:

Michael L. Faber

Homosexuality

In the 1980s, 50,000 people in the United States died of AIDS. Many people falsely believe that the AIDS problem has been conquered by new drugs. Unlike the 1980s, almost *no publicity* is given to the AIDS problem because the homosexual community and the press want to focus, instead, on the civil rights aspects of homosexuality, and paint the behavior as normal and accepted. Did you know that today 20% of all sexually active male homosexuals are infected with HIV virus, and half don't know it? This is not my opinion, but official statistics from the U.S. Government Center for Disease Control. The new drugs we have slow down, but do not eliminate the transition from HIV to AIDs. Back in the 1980s the progression from HIV infection to full-blown AIDS took two years, and now it is 12. But HIV is incurable! This means that eventually, 1 out of 5 sexually active young homosexual men will die of AIDS. A young person would have a better chance putting a bullet into a pistol and playing Russian roulette than engaging in these types of odds. Furthermore, the gay agenda has challenged our culture and legal system and led many young people to reject God outright, because they believe the world's lies about homosexuality over the truth of God's word.

Divorce

Everyone is silent about this one because we have almost as much divorce in the Church as in the world.

God intended for a man to leave his home and cleave unto his wife, and for the two to become one flesh. Instead of following God's command for marriage to be life-long and sacred, we have replaced obedience to God with our pursuit of temporary happiness. Divorce has skyrocketed to a full 50% of all marriages in America today. (Though some recent research shows it may be more like 1/3 after we take out people who are married many times.) What are the consequences? Besides the economic consequences of more women living in poverty, we see a marked increase in the chances for early sexual activity, drug addiction, and prison for youngsters raised in a fatherless household. These are true statistics, not opinions.

Drugs and Violence

More than 22 million Americans aged 12 and older – nearly 9% of the U.S. population – use illegal drugs, according to the government's 2010 National Survey on Drug Use and Health. Nearly a quarter of the population aged 12 and older participated in what the study calls binge drinking, or having five or more drinks in the same occasion, at least once in the past month. Nearly 7% of the population reported binge drinking on five days in the month before the survey. http://thechart.blogs.cnn.com/2011/09/08/study-22-million-americans-use-illegal-drugs-3/. What are we doing about this as a society? We are trying to legalize marijuana, so it will be easier, and cheaper, and more convenient to begin a lifetime of drug use.

There is a strong nexus between drug use, family violence, child abuse, murder, and property crimes, and despite this nexus almost 10% of our population is regularly abusing drugs and alcohol with all the attendant human wreckage!

Abortion

In 2009, 784,507 legal induced abortions were reported to CDC from 48 reporting areas. The abortion rate for 2009 was 15.1 abortions per 1,000 women aged 15–44 years and the abortion ratio was 227 abortions per 1,000 live births. In 2013, New York City saw more African American babies aborted than born alive. Recent news stories have decried the high death rate of infants born in Catholic run homes for unwed mothers. In one report, they found that 800 babies had died over a 40 year period and the typical voices cried out for criminal investigation and denunciation of the Catholic Church for *forced births*! As sad as these statistics are for the babies born alive in these homes that then died through poor medical care, who among these voices grieves for the hundreds of thousands of babies killed every year through legalized abortion?

Greed

In 2011, the official poverty rate was 15.0 percent in the United States. There were 46.2 million American people in poverty.

These are all absolutely true statistics gathered by government agencies, yet when I recount these statistics a number of you are thinking I am some kind of crazy, whacko, religious, extremist for bringing these things up. Don't deny it. Yet, if simply speaking the truth of facts as they exist in the government record books makes me a whacko, religious, extremist in your eyes, it is only because all the other *sane* people have stopped speaking the truth. They are covering their eyes, ears, and mouth regarding what is appearing before us all. Sane people deny the truth or ignore it, while crazy people speak it. Is that it?!!!

I do not bring us these statistics to point fingers at anyone. Many of us reading this book may be part of the above statistics in some way, through either divorce, addiction, sexual activity or some other decision we or a loved one has made in our life. No, I bring up these items to show clearly that our society is full of hurting and lost people, who are seeking happiness in all the wrong places- pursuing paths that lead to pain and misery for themselves and those around them. God is mourning because He had so much more planned.

We should mourn. We start by opening our eyes and seeing all the pain. We do not do this to condemn others, or point fingers, or to make ourselves feel better by comparison. We do this to see the truth and feel the pain God feels.

Okay, I feel the pain, now what?

As we mourn for the sin of others, what *is* the proper response? Start by prayer, and I mean fervent prayer! Pray for those in addictions. Pray for those going through divorce. Pray for the children of broken families, and pray for those in unhealthy sexual relationships. Pray for those suffering diseases that they have brought on themselves through poor choices with drugs, alcohol, or sex. Pray for the victims of sexual and physical abuse. Pray for the perpetrators. *Pray, Pray, Pray!*

Then act. All of these victims and perpetrators, all these sinners, are our loved ones, and maybe even ourselves. They are all looking for happiness, but they are making poor choices. If you love them, and you will love them as you pray for them, share with them the good news of Jesus Christ. Tell them how Christ died for them, and loves them just where they are, but loves them too much to leave them there. Don't be afraid to call sin *sin*, but offer a way out through faith in Jesus Christ. Invite them to church and into your faith community. But don't stop there ...

Whether or not they receive the gospel from you, offer to help! Help by visiting. Help by comforting. Help by babysitting. Help by loving and caring. Be part of establishing God's Kingdom in the here and now. If you pray enough, you will feel motivated to do this. But first you must mourn to feel the motivation to pray.

WHAT SHOULD BE OUR RESPONSE?

What benefit is there to mourning? Mourning brings about action. *Godly sorrow brings repentance.* If we are happy as an effect of just forgetting about all the ills of the world and sticking our head in the sand, then we will do nothing about it. If our hearts feel God's godly sorrow, we will be prompted for more prayer and action.

As we mourn, we should repent of our own personal sins.

Pray earnestly for the salvation of the lost.

Act accordingly to share the Good News with those in darkness and do what we can to lessen the impact of the sins of society.

We probably cannot greatly lessen the sin of society by anything we alone do-the hope is, that through our sharing the Good News of Jesus, as more believe, they will also yield their lives to the Savior, and this will lead to less sin.

We, by taking action to ameliorate the ill-effects of sin, share God's love for the lost, and hopefully provide attractive examples to them of what Christianity is all about, so they will be attracted to the Gospel. We are being salt and light.

HOW DOES MOURNING MAKE US BLESSED?

Jesus said, *Blessed are those who mourn.* Seeing the world through God's eyes helps us separate ourselves from our own sin and the sin of those around us. While sin gives us a temporary false happiness, holiness gives us an enduring and long-lasting happiness. We are happiest when living as God intended! As we begin to react to the pain of those around us, we also feel the blessing and the happiness of being part of the solution rather than part of the problem. Not only are we going to receive God's comfort as promised, but we will be providers of it to others as well!

REFLECTIONS:

1. Does God want us to be happy? If so, why does He tell us that we are blessed if we mourn?
2. Why does God prohibit all kinds of sexual activity which makes us happy?
3. What is the purpose of our life, if not to pursue happiness?
4. Why is mourning beneficial?
5. What did the Jews hear, when Jesus said, *Blessed are those who mourn, for they shall be comforted?*
6. How does mourning separate us from the sin around us?
7. What types of sinful and harmful activity is going on in your family or work place that you have said *nothing* about to the individuals involved?
8. Would speaking out do *any good* in the examples above?
9. Why speak out when people are just going to do what they are going to do anyway?
10. Do you ever cry when you pray?
11. Have you ever prayed fervently for sinful situations around you?
12. If you have, or do, can it do any good?

13. Are there any harmful situations around you, which you could do something to ameliorate the effects?
14. What does it mean to be the salt of the earth? How might mourning help you accomplish this?

CHAPTER 3

WHAT IS SO GREAT ABOUT BEING MEEK?

Blessed are the meek,
for they shall inherit the earth
Matt. 5:5

How many of you like to be winners? How many of you like to be losers? While we are aware that Jesus teaches *Blessed are the meek, for they shall inherit the earth,* it seems that in real life, the contrary is true. Looking around, it seems that the spoils of this life go to the sleek, not the meek! Honestly, who wins elections? Who gets the promotions? Who makes the sales? Aggression and confidence are rewarded in this society, not the opposite. But Jesus is talking about taking the long view of things, not the short view. Yes, it seems that the wicked, aggressive, and violent seem to have the advantage, right now, but we must remember that God is eternal. While we see things from this minute in time, God sees the whole picture. This little phrase is one of the *hard teachings* of Jesus, because implementing it is so contrary to our human nature, but as we will discover, it is true nevertheless.

As I have discussed in earlier chapters, the Beatitudes are *descriptive* of what Kingdom People are like. People that belong to the Kingdom are *meek*. They are not proud and arrogant. Let's discover just what exactly the word *meek* means as used by Jesus, and then look into why being meek is really preferable to the alternative.

Meek is a boring little word. Often when we hear the word, we think of a cowardly little man. This is a negative connotation in English which does not exist in the Greek. What does it mean to be *meek*, and how will being *meek* help us to be better Christians to secure the blessings promised by the Lord?

WHAT IS MEEKNESS?

Often to discover the meaning of a biblical word we need to understand how it was used in the Bible. What was Jesus thinking when He said, *Blessed are the meek?* From what context did He take this teaching, and what were the disciples hearing when the Master uttered these words?

The New Testament was written in Greek, and the Greek word for "meek" is πραυς. This word is used in Matt. 11:28-30 where Jesus declares, *Come to Me, all who are weary and heavy-laden, and I will give you rest. Take My yoke upon you and learn from Me, for I am gentle and humble in heart, and you will find rest for your souls. For My yoke is easy and My burden is light.* Notice the word *gentle*, because this word in Greek is also πραυς. Here it was translated *gentle* instead of *meek*. We learn two things from this passage. First we learn that *gentle* and *meek* are the same word in Greek. So *meek* has the same meaning as *gentle* in its original context. A meek person is gentle.

Second, we learn that Jesus describes Himself by this word. So to be meek, is to be gentle, like Jesus.

Jesus didn't just make up this teaching for His Beatitude. In fact, He quoted it from the Old Testament. It comes from Psalm 37:11, which states, *the meek will inherit the earth.* We can learn something about the context of this teaching by looking at the Psalm where it came from. Psalm 37:1-2 begins with the words, *Do not fret because of those who are evil or be envious of those who do wrong; for like the grass they will soon wither, like green plants they will soon die away.* The theme of the entire Psalm seems to be, *while the wicked seemingly prosper, they will soon be cut off, and the righteous and the meek who now have little will inherit the land.*

In this Psalm the meek are contrasted with the wicked who prosper in their wickedness and plot against the innocent. Therefore, the meek are those who do not use power and violence and conflict against others for their own aggrandizement. Rather the meek are content with what they have for the time being, secure in the knowledge that they will soon *inherit* everything. Of course to inherit something means to get it in the future, not right this minute. That is why Psalm 37:16-17 says, *better the little the righteous have, than the wealth of the many wicked, for the power of the wicked will be broken but the LORD upholds the righteous.*

What is our take away? The meek do not use power, aggression, and sin, to gain temporary advantage. They are content with what they have, and do not need to get more if it means hurting other people. The meek are also wise, because they know the Master of this Universe. They know that you cannot flout His laws for long. In the end, the meek are the ones who will endure. The meek are the ones who will inherit the possession of the goods held temporarily in the hands of the wicked. The meek take the long view, not the short view.

Another description of *meek* is being *tame*. In Matthew 21:5, it reads, *Say to the daughter of Zion, 'Behold your King is coming to you, gentle and riding on a donkey, even on a colt, the foal of a beast of burden.'* In this scripture the Greek word πραυς is translated as gentle instead of meek again, but the meaning is the same. The King riding on the donkey is gentle or meek. What can we glean from this passage?

First of all, we must realize that the *king is not weak*. He is not powerless. On the contrary, he is strong, but confident in his strength. He does not feel the need to show his power by entering town on a big white horse followed by thousands of admirers. Instead, he enters town riding on a donkey. Despite his power, he does not need to prove his greatness to everyone else. He is confident in who he is.

How many of you like dogs? Who has a little dog? Who has a big dog? I have a little dog. You know what they do all day long? Yap, yap, yap. They yap at dogs. They yap at people. They yap at squirrels, and critters, and butterflies and bees. They constantly yap to prove, mainly to themselves, how scary they are. Big dogs on the other hand just lie there. They do not bark a lot because they are confident in who they are. They have nothing to prove. Big dogs are meek, little dogs are weak.

We need to be meek, not weak.

WHAT DOES IT LOOK LIKE TO BE MEEK?

While doing research on this topic, I happened upon a quote by an anonymous Early Church Father. Early Church Fathers were Christian leaders between the time just after the Bible was written until the Fall of the Roman Empire in about A.D. 400.

This Father described a meek or gentle person as follows:

A gentle person neither provokes evil nor is provoked by evil. Charges of sin do not prevail against such persons insofar as they are not the cause of sin. The meek one is more content to endure an offense than to commit one. For unless one is unafraid of being offended, one cannot be without sin. For even as weeds are never lacking in a field, provokers are never lacking in the world. Therefore that person is truly gentle who, when he or she has been offended, neither does evil nor even thinks of doing evil. Ancient Anonymous Church Father preaching on Matt. 5:5 *Blessed are the Meek for they shall inherit the earth.*

I like that. A meek person would rather endure an offense than commit one. Meek people turn the other cheek. They are big enough to take a blow without feeling the need to respond in kind.

The opposite of this type of meekness is the false bravado of the average street-gang member who walks around looking to be offended so he can pull out his knife or gun to defend his honor. A street-gang member not only provokes others but is willing to use deadly violence if he is the recipient of the slightest provocation. He is at war with himself and everyone else. A meek person, on the other hand is at peace with himself or herself and everyone else.

A meek person holds back his or her temper. I once knew two ladies who argued all the time. While they loved each other, the slightest comment would set them bickering. Neither could allow the other to have the last word, because the last word always had some type of poke or jab, to which the other felt it necessary to respond.

I attended a seminar the other day entitled, *How to get along with Difficult People.* Difficult people have learned over their lives to get what they want by using anger and emotion rather than reason. According to the experience of the lecturer, the *worst* thing you can do is react emotionally to the provocation, since it would just add fuel to the fire, and nothing would get done. Despite this, responding in anger to their anger is the course of action that comes first to mind. After all, in our pride, we can't let them get away with insulting us, can we? And yet, psychologists will say, better take the hit, and respond calmly not only for the sake of peace but to get things done. I am reminded of the proverb, *A gentle answer turns away wrath.* Proverbs 15:1. Likewise, a meek person is more content to endure an insult than to give one. The meek get things done, even in the face of difficult circumstances.

GET OFF THE HAMSTER WHEEL!

Have you ever owned a hamster? What do they do all day? They eat, sleep, and run on their wheel, which takes them nowhere. Often, we run a hamster wheel of sorts in our daily lives.

Don't believe me? How many of you want to have a Gucci purse? How about a fancy expensive car? How about the latest i-phone? Chances are you don't need these things, but you want them for the status you think they would bring you.

I am not saying we shouldn't want comfortable or nice things, if we can afford them. I am saying, that if we are to practice meekness, we need to avoid securing status-symbols. When we buy super-expensive status-symbols we are NOT trying to secure a good and useful product, we are trying to buy the approval of men.

Meek people are humble, and they do not attempt to do things for the approval of others. Instead, they act only for the approval of our Heavenly Father. Our Heavenly Father does not approve of us more because we have purchased *status-symbol*s. Instead He looks to the *status* of our hearts. To practice meekness means to surrender in our battle to *Keep up with the Jones'*. Instead of devoting our financial resources and daily attention to remaining ahead of the fashion and technology curve, we will think about how to devote our attention to serving the Lord and our fellow man instead.

I look to the example of Pope Francis. He knows he is the Pope, but doesn't need to live in the biggest palace, wear red shoes, or drive around in the Pope-mobile. He has nothing to prove. He is meek. Instead, through his combination of gentleness, humility and tameness, he has managed to accumulate more praise and respect from others than all the red shoes, pope-mobiles and luxury apartments could ever get him!

BEING MEEK IS COUNTER INTUITIVE, BUT IT IS FOLLOWING IN THE FOOTSTEPS OF CHRIST

Why should we try so hard to be meek when it goes against the grain of who we are? We do so, because we want to follow in the footsteps of our Lord and Savior, Jesus Christ.

Think about Jesus on the Cross. He could have got off that cross and proved who He was. His enemies even taunted Him by saying, *Let him prove his power by saving himself!* Had He done so, He certainly would have saved his reputation and shown His enemies a thing or two. But that was not His goal at that moment. He had to remain meek, and remain focused, enduring even death on the cross to achieve a far greater goal. And what goal was that? To pay the price of sin for *all mankind*; even for those who taunted Him; even for those who denounced Him; even for those who pounded the nails into His hands, and poked the spear into His side. Because of the meekness of Christ, even *those people* had a chance to be saved. How much would have been lost if He had taken the opportunity to preserve His reputation instead?

Being meek is hard. Our natural desire is to defend ourselves and aggrandize ourselves in comparison to those around us. After all, competition makes us better, right? Yes, it does. But let's compete against ourselves using the standard the LORD gave us, not against others in the standard of materialism, power, and popularity.

MEEKNESS IS NOT WEAKNESS:

Meekness does not mean you cannot defend your life or those you love. Instead, I think *meekness* is somewhat related to Jesus' teaching to turn the other cheek. If someone insults you, and only your honor is at stake… turn the other cheek. On the other hand, I am a believer in having everything in balance. I am not saying if someone is going to attack you physically, that you must let them. Protect yourself and get away! Nor am I saying that if a shooter is in your school with a gun, meekness requires you to not grab the gun from the shooter. By all means grab the gun, save the lives! But meekness might dictate that you should not hog the hero limelight for the next two months.

Remember that meek king riding into town on a donkey? I bet if that king saw a robber robbing an innocent bystander alongside the road, he would jump off his donkey and prevent the crime from occurring in his kingdom. Meekness is not weakness.

Meekness is a combination of humility, gentleness and tameness, which allows you to live at peace to the greatest extent possible in this world of turmoil. It does not mean that you abdicate your responsibility to protect yourself or others in danger.

THE REWARDS ARE GREAT

As shown above, we are meek because we want to imitate our Lord. We are also meek because when we obey the Lord in this, as in all other things, we are rewarded. In Galatians 5:15, Paul states, *But if you bite and devour one another, take care that you are not consumed by one another.* The reward of the *meek* is peace. There is an old proverb which says, *Even though the Bible allows an eye for an eye and a tooth for a tooth, if we exercised this right to the fullest, the world would be full of blind and toothless beggars!* What kind of world would we live in if every wrong needed the full penalty exacted every time? Imagine how much money you would owe if you got a traffic ticket *every time* you broke a traffic law!

We need grace to survive. The meek give grace by not retaliating against every wrong they suffer. We give grace, just as, and just because, our LORD gives us grace.

We Christians exercise meekness because we love others as much as ourselves, and because we love our LORD JESUS and we want to obey Him and be like Him, and because we love peace. When we are meek, we achieve peace, and show our love.

THE MEEK WILL INHERIT THE EARTH

In Psalm 37, we are taught that the meek have *staying power*. While those who demand acceptance and power are in a constant battle with each other, and eventually will receive divine punishment...the meek stay out of the fray. While the wicked and evil and aggressive seize today, they are quickly destroyed tomorrow. On the other hand, the meek *last*.

Jesus quoted Psalm 37:11, which states, *The meek shall inherit the earth*. What does it mean to inherit the Earth?

In Psalm 37, it means that after the wicked are destroyed through their own actions, the actions of other evil people, and after the divine judgment, the meek will still be around. The wicked got all the attention and the quick money, but due to their actions they also quickly come to ruin. The Bible declares, *Better the little that the righteous have than the wealth of many wicked.* Psalm 37:16. The meek have adopted a long-term strategy. I teach anyone who will listen, *"Better the little money that you gained honestly and paid your taxes on, than a vast sum of ill-gotten gain."*

In the Old Testament, inheriting the earth was the reward of the righteous. They did not speak of heaven and hell like we do in the new covenant.

From the Christian perspective, the people who have accepted Christ as Savior and as Lord have adopted meekness as a Kingdom quality. The people of God are meek, and we will be given new bodies and new lives on the new earth when Lord has returned and all things are made new. On that day, *He will wipe every tear from their eyes. There will be no more death or mourning or crying or pain, for the old order of things has passed away.* Rev. 21:4.

We do not practice meekness in order to attain eternal life, but rather we who have attained eternal life through faith in Jesus Christ are commanded to practice meekness, as an attribute of being part of His forever family. By practicing meekness, we shine light on our Lord to others by practicing self-sacrificing love and patience in our daily lives. Through our obedience to Jesus in this matter, we attain the natural rewards of peace and fulfillment of our godly purpose in this world. Let us each follow the Lord in this matter, let us be meek, for indeed we will inherit the earth!

REFLECTIONS:

1. Have you ever known anyone who gained a fortune dishonestly? Did they keep it? If they did, what do you suppose will be their eventual reward?
2. Think of a situation where you walked away even though the other person had the last word. What

happened? Think of the opposite situation where you stayed and tried to get the last word. What happened?
3. Have you ever bought something really expensive, just to have the newest and best thing? How long did the good feelings last? Where is that item now?
4. Can you think of a situation where having the newest most expensive thing might create a barrier between you and others? How?
5. Why does Jesus want us to turn the other cheek?
6. The chapter contrasted meekness and humility with sinful and aggressive accumulation of wealth. Can you be godly and aggressive at the same time? How might this look?
7. Can one be humble and confident at the same time? How might this look?
8. When you communicate to others that you are the best, the strongest, the prettiest, what are you saying about them? How might they take that?
9. How does being meek as described in this chapter different than pacifism?
10. Why does the psalmist believe that the meek last longer than the wicked rich?

CHAPTER 4

WHY SHOULD WE DESIRE RIGHTEOUSNESS?

Blessed are those who hunger and thirst for righteousness, for they will be filled.
Matt. 5:6

I CAN'T GET NO SATISFACTION

In this life, it seems that we are all looking for something. We all desire something in order to be happy or fulfilled. But often the things we seek are different. Never is this so clear as in the marriage relationship. Often spouses feel unfulfilled in their marriage, and this often leads to divorce. A wonderful book on this topic is Gary Chapman's The Five Languages of Love. In this book he shows how different people are wired uniquely to desire different things from a relationship. Trouble in a marriage starts when one spouse is wired to desire one thing, while the other spouse is wired to desire something else. Since, we often try to show our love by giving to the other, what *we* most desire, we often leave the other unfulfilled. According to Chapman, most men and women desire either physical touch, quality time, acts of service, gifts, or words of affirmation. The trick is to provide your spouse the kind of love that he or she requires, not what *you* desire. The trouble with this hypothesis is that it doesn't always work. Lots of spouses have proceeded with a divorce anyway, even after trying out the methods of this nifty book. The problem, they have found, is that even if the other spouse tries to fulfill their desires, it is still not enough.

The truth is that many divorces happen because one spouse expects the other to satisfy a need which simply cannot be satiated. So often young married couples believe their lover will be able to *make them happy* and satisfy their desires. We have heard the line in sappy romantic movies, *You complete me*, but life often shows that this expectation is simply unrealistic. The cruel statistic that almost 50% of American marriages end in divorce bears this out. The other couples who remained married probably just learned to accept the fact that while their spouses can add value to their life, and make them happy sometimes, they are incapable of *completing* them.

Apart from the marriage scene, many individuals look for completion and fulfillment in a number of different ways. Pursuit of money and wealth is a common way that individuals seek happiness and satisfaction. But the question becomes, *How much money is really enough to satisfy me?* Is one hundred thousand dollars enough? If you are poor, you might think so. But those of us who are middle class would laugh at this number. No, one hundred thousand dollars will not make you happy. How about one million dollars? Is that much money enough to bring you satisfaction and fulfillment? For those of you who are middle class, you might think so. But the doctors and lawyers and businessmen among you who have a net worth of one million dollars or more, understand that this much money cannot bring you satisfaction. How about ten million? One billion? If so, why does Bill Gates still go to work in the morning? The truth is, if you seek after money to find self-worth, satisfaction and fulfillment, you will discover that no matter how much you make, it is not enough. Money can pay off debt and prevent certain kinds of trouble, but it cannot buy you happiness and inner fulfillment.

How about power? If you could only have influence on the world around you, wouldn't that provide a great deal of satisfaction? Often lack of power and influence over events leads us to think that if only we had power, we could be happy. People in quest for power soon realize that this too fails to satisfy. If it could satisfy, how can we explain why politicians are always running for higher office? City Councilmen want influence over the County. County Supervisors want influence over the State. State Assemblymen want to be Governor or in Congress. Everyone wants to be President. Presidents wish Congress and the media and the courts would get out of their way and let them accomplish *what really needs to be done.* No, those who have power find that no amount of power is really enough to give them satisfaction and fulfillment.

We also see other attempts to gain fulfillment through sex, drugs, and violence, entertainment, popularity, or fame, and none of these attempts lead anywhere as well. So what is it? Shall we be forever seeking and never finding?

Michael L. Faber

Jesus promised that fulfillment and satisfaction were possible. The problem is that we have been looking in all the wrong places. Jesus states, "*Blessed are those who hunger and thirst for righteousness, for they will be filled.*" Matt. 5:6. Philosopher Blaise Pascal stated, *There is a God-shaped vacuum in the heart of every man which cannot be filled by any created thing, but only by God, the Creator, made known through Jesus.* St. Augustine wrote, *Thou hast made us for Thyself, O Lord, and our hearts are restless until they rest in Thee.* In conjunction, these ideas indicate that we were created in such a way as to find perfect fulfillment only in a relationship with God. *The problem is that many of us do not know this!* Even though we might have an empty spot in our hearts in the shape of God, which only God can fill, we do not necessarily have any desire for God. We are aware only that we feel empty. Therefore, we try to fill up this emptiness with things that we know we need, or think we need, like love, money, and power. As we have already seen, love, money, power, sex, drugs, *cannot* fill this emptiness, and all we are left with is a continuing feeling of dissatisfaction. Jesus declares that if we will desire righteousness instead of these material things, we will find true satisfaction.

Righteousness is an attribute of God. Cf. Rom 3:5. When we hunger for righteousness, we are hungering for God Himself, for only He is truly righteous. When we seek righteousness to the level that Jesus describes as *hungering* and *thirsting* we are to the point of questing after God, and through this desire, when we begin filling our hearts with God's presence and His righteousness, we will attain the true fulfillment our hearts were created for. Fulfillment and satisfaction are *possible*, but only if we seek to be filled and satisfied by the right things.

A quick word about this concept. Some say that we cannot be *happy* without God, yet many non-Christians believe that they are basically happy. Furthermore, we all know plenty of unhappy Christians. Jesus does not say that you cannot be happy without God. Happiness is a temporary emotional state caused by outside stimuli. If you go out on the town with friends, fun and alcohol, you can be very happy for the time that it lasts, though deep in your heart you may still feel a dissatisfaction with your life, or a longing for *something more*. You may be unable to put your finger on just what you lack. Likewise, true Christians who find their lives filled with turmoil, illness, and poverty, might find themselves temporarily unhappy due to their circumstances, even though they have an inner peace through God. Likewise, if you are a Christian who believes in God, and attends church, and can quote scripture, you may still be quite *unfulfilled* if you are still attempting to fill your unease with money, love, romance, friendship and power, just as you did before you became a follower of Christ. Jesus says that we must *hunger* and *thirst* for righteousness in order to be filled, not just make a one-time decision at some point in our lives to believe in Him and join the Church club. **To attain true fulfillment in God, we must be ever seeking Him, and ever filling our lives with his righteousness as opposed to the**

material things that we used to chase. Seeking God will fill us with contentment that we otherwise never could have achieved; it will not necessarily make us happier than our non-Christian friends.

WHAT IS THIS RIGHTEOUSNESS THAT WE ARE TO HUNGER AND THIRST FOR?

JUSTICE:

In the New Testament, the Greek word for *righteousness* is dikaiosunē. It has two main meanings, and in the context of Jesus' teaching, either or both can fit. First of all, the word means *justice*, as in God's justice or fairness. A kingdom person desires and waits for God's justice.

Have you ever looked around at all the injustice and misery in this world, and like the prophet Habakkuk, cried out, *How much longer, Oh Lord?* The world is filled with all sorts of terrible things that grieve our hearts. Just pick up the newspaper and start reading! There is greed, corruption, unfairness, oppression, violence against the innocent, hunger, the list goes on and on. It never seems to end. The inevitable consequence of reading the news is to get upset or depressed. Why are things the way they are? Because we are all sinners.

Kingdom people long for the justice of the Lord; this is both an eschatological hope and an immediate call to action. We wait expectantly for the full justice of the LORD which will happen only at the end of days. We know that when Jesus comes back, He will judge all things. All the things wrong now will then be set right. Then, we will truly be filled. As Kingdom people, much as we may enjoy our lives in the here and now, we look forward to the Day when all things shall be made new!

Of course, as Kingdom people, we are not called to merely hunker down in our sanctuaries awaiting the End of the World! We also are called as servants of the most high to *do* justice in the Name of the LORD. Dt. 16:20 *This is what the LORD Almighty says, 'Administer true justice, show mercy and compassion to one another. Do not oppress the widow, the fatherless and the alien, or the poor. In your hearts, do not think evil of each other.'* Zech. 7:9 (In LXX the Greek wording is *Judge righteous judgment* – **Krinēdiakaio krinete**.) We who hunger and thirst for Justice should do what we can now to bring about God's justice, as part of God's Kingdom which we are now proclaiming and ushering in. "*Let Justice roll on like a river, righteousness like a never ending stream!*" Amos 5:24.

HOLINESS:

The same Greek word also means righteousness or holiness as we traditionally think about it. In Old English, righteousness was previously spelled *rightwiseness*. This is great, because being righteous in this sense is being *right with God*. It is *whatever is right or just in itself and conforms to the revealed word of God.* This might include acts of mercy. Joseph was a righteous man, because he didn't avail himself of his legal recourse of condemning Mary when he believed her to be in violation of her marriage pledge. Instead, he was merciful, and for this the Bible calls him *righteous*. Righteousness can include obedience to the Law. Many times, Christians have a hang-up about the Law of God because we think it smacks of legalism or is the opposite of grace. But the Law of God is not a bad thing, in and of itself. It is a good thing. God gave the Law to Moses, not just to confound people for thousands of years so that they would understand that they need grace, but rather to reveal to mankind what God considers good and bad. To follow the Law is to please God. God gave us the Law in His Holy Word, so that we could know what actions please Him and what actions will lead to our destruction. Where we get into trouble is if we think that through our obedience to the Law alone, we have *earned* salvation. We cannot obey the Law so well as to *earn* salvation. Salvation is given to us by grace alone. But that said, we are not to abandon or ignore the law. To understand this is to give meaning to the psalmist's words:

Blessed are they whose ways are blameless, who walk according to the law of the LORD.

Blessed are they who keep his statutes and seek him with all their heart. They do nothing wrong

And they walk in his ways... Psalm 119:1-3.

Righteousness is to seek to follow the LORD's will for our lives as set forth in his Holy Word, the Scriptures. Righteousness can also be following God's will for our lives by means revealed to us apart from Scripture. Remember when Jesus went to John to be baptized? John refused out of deference for the Lord, but Jesus insisted, declaring, *Let it be so now; it is proper for us to do this to fulfill all righteousness.* Matt. 3:15. Why? Nowhere in the Bible, up to that time, was it declared that you need to be baptized, much less that Jesus needed to be baptized by John. But Jesus knew that it was the will of His Father, and so to do it was to fulfill all righteousness. We can know the will of God by reading scripture, but God also reveals His will to us through the power of the Holy Spirit. By following the leading of the Spirit to do the will of God, we are performing acts of righteousness. A good way to think about righteousness is *being right with God.*

RIGHTEOUSNESS IS SOMETHING TO BE SOUGHT AFTER

Why should we seek righteousness? Jesus tells us to hunger and thirst after it. If we do, we will be *blessed.* He also commands, *Seek ye first the kingdom of God, AND his righteousness, and all these things will be added unto you.* Matt. 6:33. Notice we seek *God's righteousness* and not our own. Paul exhorts young Timothy, the man of God to *flee from all this (sins of the flesh) and pursue righteousness, godliness, faith, love, endurance and gentleness.* I Tim. 6:11.

Michael L. Faber

The word of God is clear in the New Testament as well as in the Old that our mission as Christians is to seek and carry out righteousness.

Righteousness can have both an active and a passive component. It is something you do, as well as something you don't do. Positively, we can carry out righteous acts, and negatively, we can be righteous by avoiding sinful acts. Despite the bad rap they were given in the Gospels, the Pharisees were quite serious about pursuing righteousness, or at least a form of it, by strict obedience to the Law of God. The Pharisees were partly righteous because they avoided personal sins, and followed ceremonial requirements of the faith. Jesus didn't fault them for this, but He condemned them because they didn't do positive acts of righteousness through love, mercy and compassion.

We don't want to be out-of-balance Christians in our pursuit of righteousness. Some Christians are all about avoiding sexual sin, not drinking, not cussing, not dancing, but they are still unhappy people, and difficult to be around. This is the pursuit of negative righteousness alone. Others help the poor, do acts of kindness, support justice, but are very loose with sexual sin and seem to have a low opinion of morality as taught by God. This active righteousness alone is also unbalanced. We need to avoid sin *and* pursue righteousness, godliness, faith, love and endurance, just as Paul told Timothy, the young man of God. **This is walking the whole walk! In other words, we are to seek God's righteousness, God's justice, God's**

will, and then do our best to conform our lives to it... as we do this, we will be filled.

WE MUST AVOID THE TRAP OF LEGALISM:

Just as the Bible clearly tells us to seek righteousness, we are told just as clearly that we will never achieve it entirely by our own efforts alone. Jesus said we must exceed the righteousness of the Pharisees to enter the kingdom of God (Matt 5:20)—this is impossible! These guys spent their whole lives trying to obey every single law. What chance do we have? Despite their best efforts to be as righteous as humanly possible, in Jesus' eyes they failed. In the Old Testament, the Prophet Isaiah states, *all of our righteous acts are like filthy rags* Isaiah 64:6. Nothing we do is entirely pure...often self-interest clouds our most wonderful actions. This why when people love you they see all the great stuff you do, but when they hate you, they see ulterior motives behind every step you take-probably they are both right! What you do is good, but usually there is a little something else mixed in. Isn't it true that when we are at our best, deep down we hope to gain some recognition or reward? Have you ever looked back years later on stuff that you did that you thought was really great, only to see the shallowness and self-centeredness of the whole venture?

While we are commanded to seek and pursue righteousness, we know from experience and from scripture that we never really attain it, entirely and purely.

Michael L. Faber

We are all like the Pharisees, *hoping to be seen by men.* Have you ever accomplished something really spiritual and great, only to stumble into sin moments later? Think about the apostle Peter. There he was recognizing the Lord Jesus as the Christ, the Son of the Living God, and receiving the keys of the kingdom, and in the next few verses he was rebuked by Christ who told him, *Get behind me Satan!* Matt. 16:16-23. Talk about spiritual whiplash!

Shall we be ever seeking but never finding? Absolutely not! JESUS says those who hunger and thirst for righteousness **shall be filled**. This is a promise. But we must attain what we desire by not going after it directly. Sometimes the more we pursue godliness, the more we receive spiritual pride, anger, and failure. To give you an example of this process, let me tell you about my little dog, Meeka. She is half Chihuahua and half Wiener dog. She is little and she is fast! Sometimes, she likes to escape from the back deck where we keep her by running under our feet when we open the gate that we installed to keep her on the deck. Through many hours of frustration, my wife and I have learned that if she escapes it is impossible to catch her. She is too fast. Not only that, she enjoys the chase. It is a game to her that she can keep up a lot longer than we can. So finally, we learned through trial and error that the best way we can catch her is to just ignore her. Eventually, she will tire of the game and walk up to us, and we can easily bend down, pick her up and put her back where she belongs.

Attaining **the righteousness needed for salvation** is much the same way. If we give it our best effort, we still are unable to be truly and consistently righteous. Knowing this, God created for us another path.

WE ATTAIN RIGHTEOUSNESS BY TURNING OUR ATTENTION TO JESUS INSTEAD:

In describing God's new plan to attain **saving righteousness,** Paul declared: "This righteousness from God comes through faith in Jesus Christ to all who believe." Rom. 3:22. It occurs when we stop trying to acquire righteousness through our own strength but instead place our faith in Christ Jesus. While we cannot be entirely *rightwise* with God through our own actions and efforts alone, by placing our faith in Jesus Christ and what He did on the Cross, God credits to us righteousness, which comes to us solely by his grace through faith. In other words, God sees our faith, and says, *Good enough!* Jesus did all the heavy lifting on the cross, by paying the price for our sin. All we need to do is believe in him, and God will reward our faith by giving us his righteousness. Like my dog, Meeka, when we look away from righteousness itself, and look to Jesus instead, saving righteousness will walk right up to us and we can pick her up.

DON'T GET DERAILED!

Saying this, about **saving righteousness**, two errant trains of thought immediately pop up which could derail God's whole plan. The first train of thought is that 1) if we are saved by grace alone, then there is no need to stop sinning; the second more recent train of thought is that 2) if Christ *did everything* on the cross to accomplish our salvation, then it is actually a sin to try and be righteous in this life anyway since it shows a lack of faith in grace alone, or Christ alone. I will deal with both of these below:

Paul dealt with the first idea directly in his letter to the Romans. *What then? Shall we sin because we are not under law but under grace? By no means!* Romans 6:15. Just because we are saved by grace, it is NOT okay to keep on sinning. Paul said, *for the wages of sin is death, but the gift of God is eternal life in Christ Jesus our Lord.* Romans 6:23. Continuing to sin deliberately is continuing in slavery to sin, and sin brings about death and all sorts of ill consequences. Jesus died to free us from slavery to sin, and instead we are slaves to God, and we need to pursue righteousness, to please God and reap holiness which leads to eternal life. Romans 6:22.

To illustrate this, imagine that your favorite basketball team traded for and received a star basketball player from another team. Your team makes the championship game, facing off against your newly acquired star's former team. As the game begins, you realize to your horror that your new star is **passing the ball to his former teammates!**

The crowd would go nuts! While the player is now owned by your team, which paid a high price for his contract, his loyalty still lies with his former team! This is how it is with us spiritually. Christ bought us for a high price. He set us free from the law of sin and death so that we could come play for his team. Why would we still want to remain loyal to the old team? Why do we still pass them the ball during the game by continually and deliberately practicing sin in our lives?

No, we were saved to be righteous, and to practice it freely and with love, without fear of our eternal destiny. In other words, we were saved by grace, and rescued from slavery to sin, so that we could practice righteousness freely without compulsion or feeling that we must do it to secure our salvation. We were not saved to practice sin without consequence.

What about the idea that we should not try to be righteous as this is actually sin because it shows lack of faith in Christ? We must understand that we do not practice righteousness to secure our salvation, for this has already been done, BUT we practice righteousness to please God, and to be what God purchased us for! Paul wrote, *"For we are God's workmanship, created in Christ Jesus to do good works, which God prepared in advance for us to do."* Ephesians 2:10. We were created to do acts of righteousness! Christ helps us do them. He does not provide an excuse or a reason to not even TRY to do them. We do good works, not out of hope of securing our salvation, which would be to bring Christ down, but to thank Him for our Salvation and to be who we were created to be!

We have faith in Christ. God reckons it to us as righteousness, and through this faith, we now play for his team, and pursue righteousness both by abstaining from sin, and pursuing positive acts of justice and mercy. We obey God. We please the Father, and in the end He will say, *Well done my good and faithful servant.*

To return to my theme throughout this series, the Beatitudes do not set conditions for salvation. The Beatitudes ***describe what Kingdom People look like.*** Kingdom people hunger and thirst for righteousness as opposed to other things. If we do not hunger and thirst for righteousness, maybe we do not belong to the Kingdom. The Beatitudes describe the rewards that will be given to His Kingdom People. Here, the result of hungering and thirsting for righteousness, as opposed to other things, is that we will be filled. As we seek the things of the LORD, He will fill us with all good things, and we indeed will find true fulfillment and true happiness. Amen.

REFLECTIONS:
1. How much money would you need before you could truly be happy?
2. Is there anything that your spouse or significant other could do, so that you would be happy?
3. Are you looking to your spouse to *complete* you?
4. How is it that seeking God can make us fulfilled?

5. What is the difference between happiness and fulfillment?
6. Do real Christians always need to be smiling? How do we know this?
7. How is striving to obey God's law different from legalism?
8. Were the Pharisees' bad? If so, why? If not, why not?
9. As a Christian do you strive more for positive righteousness or negative righteousness?
10. How could you find some more balance in your walk with God?
11. Does it show lack of faith in Christ to try to be more righteous?
12. What could you do to seek more justice righteousness?
13. If Jesus *did it all on the cross*, should Christians continue to hunger and thirst for righteousness? Why?
14. According to Ephesians 2:10, why were we created?
15. What is our reward for hungering and thirsting for righteousness?

CHAPTER 5

BLESSED ARE THE MERCIFUL, FOR THEY SHALL OBTAIN MERCY
Matt. 5:7

Now we shall discuss the fifth Beatitude, *Blessed are the merciful, for they shall obtain mercy.* Honestly, when I first read this Beatitude it seemed kind of boring. Maybe it was a rephrase of the idea that we need to show forgiveness if we want to be forgiven. As I studied it more, I found it quite deep.

WHAT DOES IT MEAN TO BE MERCIFUL?

Often when we hear the word *mercy*, we think of it in a judicial sense. We think of receiving mercy as not receiving the punishment we deserve. Almost like *Please your honor, give me a break.* This is how we use the word most commonly in modern English.

The Greek word for mercy in this verse is **Eleos**. In a biblical sense, this Greek word, is probably closer to the modern word compassion. In fact in many other verses containing the word, **Eleos**, translators translate it to say *compassion* or *pity* instead of *mercy*.

Remember the ten lepers that were cleansed? They cried out *Jesus, Master, have mercy (pity) on us!* They weren't asking for Jesus to forgive them but to help them in their moment of need. Mercy is more like lending a hand than giving a break. Giving a break is also like exercising grace, or unmerited favor. We do not receive the punishment we deserve because of God's grace. Mercy and grace are interlinked concepts. Both give something that is undeserved. They both spring from the internal love of the giver to provide for the needs of the recipient. While grace is not giving someone the punishment they otherwise deserve, *mercy* is where *God meets us in the time of our distress.*

I call to the Lord in my distress, and he answers me. Psalm 120:1.

Likewise, when the rich man was burning in hell, he cried out *Father Abraham have mercy (pity) on me and send Lazarus to dip the tip of his finger in water and cool my tongue, because I am in agony in this fire.* Luke 16:24. He was in great distress. He did not ask to be forgiven for his sins, or even to be released from hell. All he wanted was some water from Lazarus, because extreme thirst was his point of need. What he asked for was an act of compassion to relieve him in his distress. In old times, we called these *acts of mercy.*

Have you heard of Mother Theresa? The group she founded is called the Sisters of Mercy, not because they go around getting people off criminal sentences they deserve, but because they are dedicated to performing acts of compassion and assistance for the poorest of the poor.

In the Beatitudes, Jesus describes what His Kingdom People look like. Kingdom People are merciful. They show acts of mercy to those in distress.

Michael L. Faber

In one of his most famous parables, the Parable of the Sheep and the Goats, Jesus shows us what merciful people look like. In the 25th chapter of Matthew, Jesus tells us how when the Son of Man comes in glory with his angels, He will sit on His throne and gather the nations before him. He will separate them like sheep from the goats. He will put the sheep on his right hand and the goats on his left hand. Then he will declare, *Come you who are blessed by my Father: take your inheritance, the kingdom prepared for you since the creation of the world. For I was hungry and you gave me something to eat. I was thirsty and you gave me something to drink. I was a stranger and you invited me in. I needed clothes and you clothed me. I was sick and you looked after me. I was in prison and you came to visit me.* Matt. 25:34-36.

To those on his left, he will declare, *Depart from me,* because they did not do acts of mercy in their lifetime. When each group ask him whenever they ever had time to do or not do any of these acts of mercy for Him, Jesus will declare, *Whatever you did for one of the least of these brothers of mine, you did for me.* Matt. 25:40.

Notice the acts that mark those who receive the kingdom in this parable; feeding the hungry, giving water to the thirsty, providing shelter to the traveler, distributing clothes to the poor, spending time visiting the sick and the imprisoned. These are all acts of mercy and compassion. Kingdom people are merciful. Merciful persons, do these things. Merciful people are sheep and not goats. Merciful people are blessed or happy, precisely because they are granted the Kingdom!

WHY IS MERCY IMPORTANT?

Mercy Increases the Effectiveness of Evangelism

There is an old adage which my mentor, pastor William Goddard, taught me, *People don't care what you know, until they know how you care.*

Showing mercy, as part of your daily routine, is an essential part of your evangelical witness!

I came across a true story on the internet that illustrates the importance of mercy in evangelical witness! Evidently, a benefactor with great wealth decided to go out in the city and hand out money to random people. He approached a man and put $200.00 into his hands. The man objected, *I didn't earn this.* The benefactor insisted, *I can see you are a good man.* The man broke down in tears. What the benefactor didn't know was that this man was a drug addict. As you know, drug addicts do anything they can to get more drugs. This drug addict had a child by a woman who was not his wife, and earlier in the week, the addict had sold his child's Christmas presents from under the tree, to get a fix of drugs. This made the child's mother quite angry and when she threatened to leave him, he begged her to stay. He apologized but said he couldn't help it. He had tried drug counseling before and it didn't work. She pressed him, *You don't believe in God, but why don't you try something new, and pray to God for assistance.* In order to appease her, he reluctantly mouthed a prayer for God to reveal himself and provide him some help. This was the night before the benefactor approached him.

Now most of us would not hand $200.00 to a stranger, especially one who might look like a drug addict. The businessman followed a hunch, however, and presented this man with an unwarranted gift. The addict broke down in tears because he knew this random gift was a sign. The sign showed him that God was real and that He cared. Now the addict is a believer, and ready to attempt drug counseling again, this time with God on his side!

Of course, the businessman could have just approached the addict and handed him a gospel tract with verses from the Bible. This might have had an effect, but truthfully, the addict was in need of money and compassion at that time, and this act of financial kindness struck him to the heart! It was unexpected. It was undeserved. It showed pure love. Because of this act of mercy, the addict was able to receive the grace of God.

Once I was out passing water to homeless people on a hot Summer day. After they received the water, I asked if they would like a copy of my prior book *Meditations on the Lord's Prayer*. While some of them received it joyfully, one of the homeless men replied, *Christian literature, I've got plenty of, but this water really helps!* Often people need to experience God's love first, before they are ready to hear about it.

Jesus Himself spent His entire ministry *both* preaching the truth, *and* doing acts of mercy, reaching out to people where they were.

A human being is body, soul (emotions) and spirit. Yes, we must minister to the needs of the spirit by proclaiming the truth from God's word, but to minister to the whole person, we must also minister to the soul or emotions by our visiting in times of distress, and to the body, by providing food and clothing when necessary to the poor. This is what the saved do. These are acts of mercy that assist the child of God to minister to others, completely. This is what shows people that we care.

Mercy is not merely income redistribution to obtain some socialist equality of wealth; rather it is meeting the needs of others in love, so as to bring them to the Father!

MERCY REVEALS THE NATURE OF GOD

When we perform acts of Mercy, we are sharing with people the Nature of God! What is the nature of God? *But you O Lord, are a compassionate (merciful) and gracious God, slow to anger, abounding in love and faithfulness.* Psalm 86:15.

This little epigram about the character of God appears again and again in the Old Testament. You notice that God is shown as *both* merciful and gracious. Mercy meets us where we are physically and emotionally, grace causes

God to forgive our sins. *I like to think Mercy meets the needs of body and soul, so grace can give life to the Spirit.* So often we focus on the grace of God, because we are fixated on eternal life, and we forget about the mercy of God, in meeting our needs in this life. God, according to this OT formula is both merciful and gracious.

These Scriptures reveal that God is a God of Mercy as well as a God of Grace. He delights in meeting the needs of people where they are at. He does not do this just to solve our problems or make our lives easier, but to draw us closer to Him! He shows us mercy, so as to bring us into closer relationship!

We cry out, for some physical or emotional need, and the LORD is happy to meet us there, but He also wants to use this event to draw us into spiritual wholeness!

I go back to the story of the ten lepers. In that story, they were suffering from the physical need of leprosy. They cried out to the Lord Jesus, *Have mercy on us!* They wanted to be healed, physically. Jesus performed the miracle they desired, but only one came back to give thanks. To this one, he declared *Arise and go, your faith has made you well.* Luke 17:11-19. In Greek, literally it says *Your faith has saved you* [he pistis sou seswken se]. While the context, picked up by all the biblical translators, indicates a physical healing, the actual Greek word indicates maybe something more was going on, at least with the one who returned. Jesus didn't make this comment to the others! At least for the one, maybe something spiritual was happening along with the physical healing.

They cried out for physical healing but God did not want to leave them there, He reached down to provide spiritual as well as physical comfort!

At our church, we had a Buddhist lady who immigrated to the United States to be with her husband. She attended church on a weekly basis, and many times she was approached by would be evangelists who tried to lead her to the Lord. I, myself, directed a few sermons her way, but none struck home. Finally, her husband became very ill. Members of the church came around both of them, and tended to her needs, helped her pay the bills, and drove her to visit her husband. One individual, Mr. Vien, helped her almost every day during her husband's last few months on earth. She began to bargain with God, promising that if God would heal her husband, she would become a Christian. Then, unexpectedly, her husband took a turn for the worse. God denied the deal. She could have become embittered and walked away, stating, *I knew God was not real!* But instead, on the night before his expected death, she gave her heart to the Lord anyway! Why? Because she was won over by the love shown to her by the people of the Church. She could see who God was, through His people. Indeed, God is a merciful God. Because she could see that mercy, she was able to receive His grace.

We see who God is, through His Son Jesus. People of the world see who Jesus is, through us.

Michael L. Faber

BEING JESUS TO THE WORLD:

Jesus commands, *Be merciful, just as your Father is merciful.* Luke 6:36. Just like earlier, He commands us to forgive the sins of others if we wish to be forgiven. As Christians, it is not our job only to receive the grace of God so we can have our sins forgiven and go to heaven. Rather, we are to be *conduits* of God's love and God's mercy for a lost and dying world. Our job is not just to believe and be forgiven, but to believe, then go out and show the world the nature of God by forgiving others and showing others mercy, just as God does.

We embody the Spirit of God. When we are saved, we go forth to *be Jesus* to those around us. When they see forgiveness and mercy in action through us, they can better understand and better believe God, and better receive His mercy and forgiveness for themselves! Like many have said before, we may be the only Bible some people ever read. They won't pick up the Scriptures, and they certainly won't attend our service, but they know that we are Christians, and they are judging who God is, by how we act in our daily lives! Lord, help us to be worthy ambassadors for you!

When we perform acts of mercy in the Name of Jesus Christ, yes, we help the poor, we visit the lonely, or comfort the afflicted, and all these things have value in and of themselves, but at the same time **we are acting as a conduit of God's love to the world and spiritual fruit cannot help but grow!**

Some might object saying *compassion* and *mercy* are not limited to Christians. I have seen Buddhists, Muslims and atheists perform acts of compassion. This proves nothing, because each of us, regardless of our religion, was created by the same God, in His image! *Compassion* and *mercy* are attributes hidden deeply in the hearts of all mankind. This is because all men were created in the image of God, and God is *merciful.* As Christians, we are commanded to dig deep into ourselves, and practice mercy, and make it stronger through practice so that it comes easier.

While all men are created in the image of God, and all have some degree of mercy and compassion, we have the Spirit of God living in us, when we are saved! Since we have the Spirit in us, we need to allow Him to work through us, to shine His light on a dark and lonely world!

WHAT MERCY DO THE MERCIFUL OBTAIN?

This Beatitude states, *Blessed are the merciful, for they shall obtain mercy.* We have discussed how the entire set of Beatitudes describes the attributes of Kingdom People, but this beatitude also promises a specific reward to those who practice mercy. Does showing mercy and doing acts of compassion actually guarantee that you will receive the same in return? My personal experience leads me to say that just because you are nice to a **particular** person does not guarantee that said **particular** person will be nice back to you if the tables are turned. Sometimes the opposite is true.

Have you ever heard the secular saying, *No good deed goes unpunished?* Unfortunately, sometimes when we show acts of kindness to others, due to their shame or mental illness, they react badly to us. More than once, I have been yelled at or verbally abused by homeless people or teenagers or old people that I was trying to help. Momentarily, this makes me want to quit, but I remember the biblical admonition, *Never tire of doing what is right.* 2 Thess. 3:13. Paul would not have commanded this if doing right was easy and full of natural rewards. Instead, we must, if we are to continue to be faithful, look at the big picture.

What is the big picture? Paul says, *A man reaps what he sows.* Gal. 6:7. If we sow to please the sin nature we reap destruction, and if we sow *to please the Spirit, from the Spirit will reap eternal life.* Gal. 6:8. When we perform acts of mercy to help others, we are doing so in obedience to God, to act as conduits of His love for a lost and hurting world. When we do these things, we are sowing to please the Spirit as opposed to our own fleshly desires. Sometimes we get slapped down by the very ones we are trying to help, but Paul continues, *Let us not become weary in doing good, for at the proper time we will reap a harvest if we do not give up.* Gal. 6:9.

What is that harvest? I do believe that when we do good works for others, we will receive more good from others than if we had done nothing. This is a natural principle. It is the same as if I walk around with a good attitude: more good things happen to me than if I walk around with a sour disposition. Hindus call this karma. The Bible refers to it as sowing and reaping. It is just as natural as the law of gravity. Help, and you will be helped. Probably not by the very people you help, but certainly by others. This is worldly sowing and reaping but a true principle nonetheless, and one we should be happy to live by. When we show mercy to those around us, the laws of Nature will ensure that we live happier and more blessed lives than if we withheld our acts of kindness.

Then, as is shown by Jesus in His discourse on the Sheep and the Goats, there is an otherworldly or eternal reward system in place as well. That is the Day of Judgment. On this Day, we will all stand before the King on his throne. God will separate the sheep from the goats. The sheep were those who practiced mercy, and the goats were those who did not. This is the harvest that Paul referred to in Gal. 6:9. In that last Judgment day, the merciful did receive mercy from the King. If we are kingdom people, and if we have saving faith, we must practice mercy as naturally as if we breathe. Sometimes this is hard, but as Kingdom People, it is our job to usher in God's Kingdom here and now. One of the most effective ways to do this is by practicing mercy. Amen?

REFLECTIONS:
1. What is the difference between mercy and grace?
2. What is the character of God?
3. Does the parable of the Sheep and the Goats indicate that we must earn our salvation?
4. Are saved people Sheep or Goats?
5. What is the character of a Sheep in Jesus' parable?
6. What kinds of ways can you show mercy to those around you?
7. How does mercy assist us in our evangelism?
8. Should we be merciful even to those who we know will never become Christians? Why?
9. Have you ever shown mercy to someone only to have them turn around and harm you in some way? How does this make you feel? Should you continue showing mercy in the future? Why?
10. Has anyone ever shown you mercy at a key time in your life?

CHAPTER 6

SEEING GOD IN A BUSY WORLD

Blessed are the pure in heart, for they shall see God.
Matt. 5:8

We continue on our journey through the Beatitudes to see the type of people Jesus says are happy. These people are Kingdom People. Jesus tells us what it means to be a citizen of the Kingdom of God, and what the rewards of Kingdom citizenship are. According to this next Beatitude, happy people have *pure hearts* and as a result they can *see God*. What does it mean to have a pure heart? And what does it mean to *see God*. We will examine these things, but first let's start with the definition of what it means to *see God*.

WHAT DOES IT MEAN TO SEE GOD?

The Bible says, *No one has ever seen God, but God the One and Only, who is at the Father's side, has made Him known.* John 1:18. And again, *No one has ever seen God; but if we love one another, God lives in us and His love is made complete in us.* I John 4:12. Is the Bible in contradiction? Jesus says, *Blessed are the pure in heart, for they shall see God* and yet John says no one has seen God. Does this mean Jesus is mistaken or that John is mistaken? Some might try to reconcile this apparent contradiction with a line like *No one is without sin, therefore no one is pure,*

Michael L. Faber

so none have seen God. We will see God in heaven after we have received our resurrection bodies. Growing up, I heard much teaching like this. Essentially, the Beatitudes were nothing but an affirmation that the believers would go to heaven after they died. While this is true, honestly it gives a very thin interpretation to the deep meaning of the Beatitudes. As I have taught throughout this book, and in my last one, *Meditations on the Lord's Prayer*, when we are saved, we are saved *into* eternal life with God. Eternal does not start in the future, it begins right now! The Beatitudes teach us how we are to live as kingdom people right now, and tell us the rewards for living so. It is possible right now to *see God* in the way Jesus intended us to take the expression. This way is different from the way John used his term *seeing God*.

We must conclude that *seeing God* as used in this Beatitude is a term of art. Of course no one has *seen God* with his or her eyes because *God is Spirit.* John 4:24. You can't *see* a Spirit. We must not take Jesus' words in this case to mean literally that we will see God with our eyes, but rather think of it a little more expansively. When we see something, we know what it is about, gain a certain understanding. Likewise *seeing God* can be understood as knowing about God, becoming familiar with Him, and understanding His will. The *pure in heart* will hear Him, understand Him, be close and intimate with Him, and know Him. When you go *see* a friend, you are not going to examine him or her with your eyeballs, but you are going to spend time in his presence, in proximity and in communication.

The pure in heart are able to spend time with God in His presence and communicate with Him. And of course, communication is a two-way street. It implies both speaking to God as well as hearing from God.

Are you ready, my friend, to go *see God?* If so, then Jesus says you need to have a pure heart.

WHAT DOES IT MEAN TO HAVE A PURE HEART?

As we will see, being *pure in heart* implies a singleness of purpose, as well as a ritual and/or moral purity. St. Augustine wrote *'Blessed are the pure in heart, for they shall see God.' How foolish, therefore, are those who seek God with these outward eyes, since He is seen with the heart! As it is written elsewhere, 'And in singleness of heart seek Him.' For that is a pure heart which is a single heart.*

BEING PURE OF HEART MEANS DESIRING ONE THING

For those of you who have gold jewelry, you know that having something made from 24 karat gold is more valuable than having something made from 14 karat gold. This is because 24 karat gold is more nearly *pure* gold, while the designation 18 karat or 14 karat gold implies that it is not *pure* but mixed with alloys for industrial purposes. Likewise *pure* water is a liquid that contains only water, while impure water contains other ingredients mixed into the water. Have you ever turned on the water faucet and seen brown water come out of the tap? While that water may be technically safe to drink, it is not very appealing because it is *not* pure water, but mixed with other minerals.

A heart that is *pure* is one that is focused on only one thing, and not distracted or divided. When Jesus speaks of an individual with a *pure heart*, He is speaking of a person whose heart is solely focused on God and not distracted by other things. He is speaking of a heart that does not suffer from divided loyalties.

If a Christian wants to see God or hear His voice, or be in His presence, she needs to learn to do away with distractions that so frequently pull her heart away from the prize.

One of the marks of modern life is that things are getting busier and busier and more and more hectic. There truly is little down time where we can be alone in our thoughts and alone with our God. Even in those moments that traditionally yielded down time such as when we are in the car driving, or waiting in line, we can now be distracted by iPods, radios, and smart phones. Our schedules fill up with more and more activities, but we truly never want to waste even a moment! We want more and more. But in all honesty, in the midst of all this hectic business, when do we have time for God?

We are reminded of the story in the Old Testament when the Prophet Elijah came out of a powerful showdown with the wicked Queen Jezebel and her prophets of Baal. While Elijah was the victor, he was spiritually, emotionally, and physically spent. God told him to meet Him on a mountain. Elijah made his way to the mountain, and sat in a cave, waiting for the LORD to show Himself. Then Scripture tells us there was a mighty wind, with such fearsome power that rocks were cracked! But God was not in it. Then there was a powerful earthquake that shook the land! But God was not in it. Finally, a fire fell from the sky, scorching everything in its path! But God was not in it. Then the Bible tells us that there came a soft-wind, like a gentle whisper, and Elijah pulled his cloak over his face, and stood up at the mouth of the cave to meet the LORD. He recognized that the voice of the LORD was in the gentle wind, and not in all the crashing fiery things that we often expect if we are to hear from God! Don't get me wrong, the LORD is fully capable of putting on a pyrotechnic display if He so desires, and He has done it a *few* times in Scripture; but most of the time, when we hear from God, it is in the whispers and not the explosions.

Michael L. Faber

GOD IS MORE FREQUENTLY SEEN AND HEARD IN THE GENTLE SLENDER WHISPERS THAN THE CRASHING OF GREAT THINGS

We are often conditioned to expect that if God communicates it will be in some explosive manner such as happened to Moses in the burning bush or the parting of the Red Sea. How often does this really occur? More often, we are more like Elijah than Moses. Elijah took time out of his busy schedule to seek the presence of God, and it was not found in the rock-shattering wind, the terrible earthquake, or the scorching fire. *After the fire came a gentle whisper. When Elijah heard it, he pulled his cloak over his face and went out and stood at the mouth of the cave.* I Kings 19:12-13 (NIV).

Can we recognize the still small voice of God? We must learn to listen. God is with us all the time, but we must take the time to recognize Him. Let me give you an example. Did you know that stars shine even in the day? If you go outside in the daytime, you will not see them. Their light is drowned out by the sunlight. Because of the overpowering light of the sun, when we look to the rest of the sky, all we see is blue. Despite this illusion, the stars are still there, and they are still shining. We won't see them however until the sun sets and stops blinding us to the starlight. It is the same way with God. He is always speaking to us, but the clamor of our own desires, of the material things, and worldly cares, and our personal sin masks His voice so we do not hear it.

I don't know why God chooses to present Himself in this way. Certainly He has the power to come with fire and smoke and noise to capture everyone's attention in spite of what they are doing. This is how it will be at the Second Coming of Christ. But until then, God delights in subtlety. He presents Himself only to those who truly seek Him in faith. Maybe this is His way of weeding out His true followers. I don't know. With this in mind, however, we know that God frequently presents Himself in subtlety and quietness.

Ralph Waldo Emerson once wrote, *Let us be silent that we may hear the whisper of God.*

The voice of God may come to you as a random thought, or an illustrative event that occurs to you that makes a light bulb go on

Once when Mother Teresa was riding a train and contemplating the extreme poverty of the people of Calcutta, she saw a vision of Jesus hanging on the Cross, saying the words, *I thirst*. Nothing more. But as she contemplated this vision, she felt as if Jesus was thirsting to love His people, and thirsting for them to love Him, and that it would be her job to bring His love to the poorest of the poor in Calcutta. No great miracle here, but a simple vision and a few words, yet God was speaking to her in this simple manner, setting off one of the greatest Christian missions in the 20th Century.

God often speaks to us in events and impressions, and coincidences, and feelings and impressions. The key to hearing God's voice is to learn to recognize it!

My Sheep listen to my voice! John 10:27.

Just as the baby learns to hear the voice of its mother, so must we learn to recognize the still small voice of God.

What does hearing the voice of God look like? If you know anything about me, you know I spend a lot of time on Facebook. You also know that while at times I can be generous, I also have a natural inclination to guard my pocketbook! One day, I was on Facebook interacting with a pastor friend of mine when I saw the face and words pop up from a pastor in Africa on his page. I heard the voice of God clearly say to me *Make friends with that man!* Immediately, I resisted, thinking, *If I do it's going to cost me. He is going to hit me up for donations.* God repeated the words, *Make friends with that man!* So I obeyed. Yes, I did make some donations, but as it turns out, that was not the apparent plan of God. Almost immediately, a Facebook friend of that pastor from India saw my picture on his African friend's page, and requested me to be his friend. Knowing the connection, I agreed so I could see what God had in store.

This Indian Pastor's name was Pastor Gabriel Muppidi. He wanted a copy of a manuscript I had written on the Lord's Prayer, so he could translate it. I agreed. Again, I thought, *This is going to cost me.* Again, I made some donations to help with this and that. (As you can see, I am still working on the *cheerful* part of *cheerful giving*). Pastor Gabriel Muppidi would give me periodic updates of his progress in translating my manuscript as I myself worked on publishing the English version. Eventually, there came the moment of truth, when I was requested to wire $675.00 for printing the Indian edition. I was suspicious because there are so many internet scams going on, and I prayed about it. I heard the LORD say, *Go ahead, trust him.* So I sent the money. Soon, he had printed 1000 copies of *Meditations on the Lord's Prayer* in the Telugu language! I received pictures and reports from multiple sources as he passed these books around to home church pastors in South Eastern India, helping them with their ministries. He also used them as valuable tools in his personal evangelism. He followed up by translating into four different Indian languages my Christmas sermon, *This Christmas What Will We Give to Him?* He passed out 20,000 copies of these gospel tracts. He followed up with another 1000 copies of *Seven Words from the Cross*, and I am confident will do likewise with this book. He has proven to be a trustworthy and dedicated partner in our literature ministry in South Eastern India!

Now get this. I have never been to India. Before I met this pastor, I had never heard of the Telugu language. My heart has always been directed to Vietnam. But for some unknown reason, God wanted my works published in India. He wanted me to get involved with home church pastors in India. He spoke to me in a voice in my head, saying but a few words. *Make friends with that man.* And

Go ahead, trust him. I heard this voice, and I obeyed, and there has been magnificent fruit as a result!

The key is listening and learning to *discern the voice of God.* Jesus says, *My sheep hear my voice.* John 10:27. Pray about it when it comes to you to see if it is really God who is speaking. Do not be hesitant to hear the voice of God. *Do not quench the Spirit; do not despise prophetic utterances. But examine everything carefully; hold fast to that which is good...* I Thess. 5:19-21. Also do not be too anxious to believe that every thought that pops into your head is from God. When God speaks to you this is a prophetic utterance, but we must *test the spirits* to see if they are really from God. I John 4:1.

So we know that when we hear from God, it is more likely to be a whisper than a shout. We know He may speak to us in visions or thoughts or impressions. We know, to hear Him, we need to have a pure heart that is devoted to *wanting* to hear His voice.

WE MUST LEARN TO ELIMINATE DISTRACTIONS

As we begin our quest to hear from God, we need to start by setting aside some quiet time dedicated to *being with* God. I recommend taking at least 15 minutes out of your schedule and finding a place with the least amount of distraction. While a person of great spiritual maturity may be able to hear God's voice amidst the clamor of daily life, thoughts and cares, most of us cannot. This is why when Jesus was preaching the parable of the seeds, He mentioned seeds which were not very productive because they *fell among the thorns which grew up and choked the plants.* Matt. 13:7. These seeds were not very fruitful, and when Jesus was asked to explain, He said *The one who received the seed that fell among the thorns is the man who hears the word, but the worries of this life and the deceitfulness of wealth choke it, making it unfruitful.* Matt. 13:22. This verse has many applications to our spiritual life, but my point here is that as we are trying to receive the word of God in prayer, the worries and distractions of life can choke our fruitfulness. More on this later.

Like our earlier discussion of the starlight being overpowered by the sun, the voice of God is available to us all day, but the noise and clamor of our worries and busyness drown out His presence, and we are unaware that He is there. If we will take the time, we can access Him anytime we like!

The distractions of our lives are like the sunlight that drowns out the starlight. These distractions are of many types. Distractions can be anything that draws our attention from the Lord. They can be good things – such as fulfilling family and work duties. They can be neutral things – such as general busyness, noise, music, TV. They can be bad things—such as un-repented sin in your life.

So we want to hear from the Lord, let's get control of these distractions. First the easy stuff. Get rid of noise and busyness by finding a quiet place away from the duties that take up your time. Maybe a tree outside, a closet, a chapel at your church, your car at lunch time, a bench. Any place will do as long as it is away from your normal place of business. Turn off any media device. Cell phones, TV's, radios. Hit that off button! Now spend some time with God.

Guess what? Now that you have turned off your devices, and found that quiet place, once you have gone through your prayer list, now thoughts are going to start distracting you. Yes! Thoughts of everything in your life will start to intrude into your prayer time. Your first inclination might be to put them out of your mind, because you want to *meditate on the LORD!* You can try putting them out, but perhaps they are persistent. Instead of struggling with these thoughts, **use spiritual jujitsu!** Pull them in! Pray about *these things* that your brain or the devil insists on putting in your brain. Whatever they are! Lustful thoughts, worries about work or family, grief, fear…take *these things and make them the subject of your prayer!!!*

THE PURE IN HEART CONTINUALLY REPENT OF SIN

The last type of distraction we need to deal with, which I put last for organization purposes, but which I recommend you deal with *first* in your prayer time is un-repented sin. Sin is a distraction which separates us from the presence of God. Think about it. Just after you deliberately sin, how much do you *feel like* getting into the presence of God? Just like Adam and Eve, you want to hide instead, because you realize you are naked!

Jesus describes the type of person that sees God. They are those who are *pure of heart*. The word in Greek is **Katharoi te kardia**. Those whose hearts are morally and ritually pure.

According to the Danker Bauers Greek-English Lexicon on the New Testament, the Greek noun **Kaθaros** implies one who is both ritually and morally pure. How can we be ritually and morally pure? Doesn't the Bible teach us that *There is no one righteous, not even one?* Romans 3:10. Is Jesus now contradicting Paul? Again, we have a contradiction only if we read the terminology too literally. Yes, it is true, there is no one absolutely without sin, not even one. But again, Jesus must not mean this so literally, or He would not have bothered to teach it to us in this Beatitude.

To start with understanding what Jesus may have been getting at, again we remember that to be *pure* or **Kaθaros** meant to be **ritually pure**. In OT times, the altar of the Temple was presumed to be ritually impure because of the sin of the people that had contaminated it. The priest *purified* the golden altar ritually, by sprinkling blood of the sacrificial animal over the top of it. While not very sanitary, the altar was now *pure*. Leviticus 4:7, 16:18.

Likewise, when we are unsaved, we are ritually impure because of original sin and actual sin which has contaminated us in the eyes of God. When we receive Christ as our Savior, we allow His blood to cleanse us from our sins and make us ritually pure before God. *Everyone who believes in him receives forgiveness of sins through His name.* Acts 10:43. *How much more then, will the blood of Christ, who through the eternal Spirit offered himself unblemished to God, cleanse our consciences from acts that lead to death, so that we may serve the living God.* Hebrews 9:14.

THE FIRST STEP TO BECOMING PURE OF HEART IS TO ALLOW YOUR HEART TO BE CLEANSED OF SIN BY THE BLOOD OF CHRIST, AND THIS IS ACCOMPLISHED BY PRAYING FOR HIM TO BECOME YOUR SAVIOR AND LORD!

To be *pure* or **Kaθaros** also means to be *morally pure*. While we are made ritually pure at our initial salvation, we are also to be *morally pure* if we want to enjoy intimacy with God. While the Bible teaches that all sin and fall short of the glory of God, yet Jesus teaches that the *pure in heart* will see God. We must conclude that being *pure of heart* does not mean that one is entirely without sin, since no one can be. We must learn to think in terms of degrees and not absolutes, to understand this.

For instance, a person whose life is marked by sin, violence, corruption, greed and self-centeredness is certainly not seeking God, and unlikely to hear His voice, unless God had a specific message for him. Such a person is *not* pure of heart. A person who is pure of heart is one whose life is not marked by the practice of sin, violence, corruption, greed and self-centeredness. Rather, a person of pure heart is seeking to live a God-centered life and is straining to hear the voice of God.

Sometimes we hear so much preaching about how all have sinned, and no one is pure, and every man is depraved, and that there is no difference in sin before God, that we forget that God really does want us to do our best to obey His laws! Such preaching is designed to make the point that none of us can earn our own salvation without God's grace, because none of us can obey the law entirely. If we miss just one point, no matter how small, we are a lawbreaker and have blown it before God. The answer to that point is the blood of Christ which atones for all sin, and allows us to approach the throne of grace with confidence. That discussion concerns our initial salvation, but should *not be confused with how God wants us to live once we are saved!* He has laws for a reason, and He sets forth His laws in the Bible not just to make the perverse point that they are too hard to keep, and therefore we know we need a Savior. No! He set forth His laws to teach us how to live abundant lives. It is for this reason Christians are not encouraged to go forth and lie and rape and steal and kill, and backbite and gossip, and then kick back and say, *Your grace is sufficient for me!* No! Now that we are saved, we are to *Live as children of light (for the fruit of the light consists in all goodness, righteousness and truth).* Ephesians 5:9. We are commanded to *find out what pleases the Lord. Have nothing to do with the fruitless deeds of darkness...* Ephesians 5:10. The Lord tells us clearly what pleases Him in His law. Often when we break the laws of God, we feel guilt, and we feel separated from God's love (though this is not true). We do not want to pray, but we want to ignore God so that our feelings of guilt will be diminished.

IN OTHER WORDS, SIN IS JUST ANOTHER REAL BIG DISTRACTION. IN ESSENCE SIN IS WHEN WE TAKE OUR FOCUS OFF GOD AND PUT IT ONTO OTHER THINGS THAT ARE HARMFUL TO US AND OUR SPIRITUAL WALK WITH GOD.

When we receive forgiveness for sins through Jesus, we become *ritually pure*. But to continue our walk towards purity, we must actually repent of our sins and do our best to keep our lives free from them. Paul states it clearly to the Corinthians who regularly practiced sin…He entreats them, *Since we have these promises, dear friends, let us purify ourselves from everything that contaminates body and spirit, perfecting holiness out of reverence for God.* 2 Cor. 7:1. Here he uses the Greek verb **Kaθarizw** which is related to the noun Jesus used to express the pure of heart. The pure of heart purify themselves continually of those things that contaminate body and spirit in order to perfect holiness… Why do they do this? Out of reverence for God!

Our goal and our walk is to ascertain God's will for our lives and then to perform it. Our pleasure is to hear God's voice and to realize that He has a plan for us. Our ability to do this depends on being pure of heart. To be pure of heart, we must have our hearts focused on God. We also need to be cleansed of sin, which is accomplished by the blood of Jesus on the cross, and through continual confession and repentance.

How do we become pure of heart? We purify our hearts by removing the taint of sin which separates us from God. Now when we are first saved, we feel all fresh, pure and excited. If you had a *born again* experience as a teen or an adult, you know what I am talking about. Unfortunately, as life went on, you began to make poor choices, sinning and falling away on this point and that. Perhaps you sinned within a day or so of your salvation experience, and little by little, those feelings of God's closeness began to drift away.

Don't get me wrong. Anything new has the potential of becoming less exciting as you get used to it. But also, as you began to sin, and make choices to put other things before God, your relationship began to deteriorate.

How many of you have a dog? When you pour the dog a nice fresh bowl of water, how pure is it? How clean? It looks great. Now give it a day or so. What does it look like now? Didn't you fill that bowl with fresh clean water? Yes you did, but over time, dust and dirt settled into it from the atmosphere. Bacteria floated in through the dog's snout, and who knows what other animals. Little by little, the stuff of life destroyed that pure water, and now you need to pour it out and get some fresh water! Such is our spiritual lives. We start out pure, but little by little we make poor choices, and other factors intrude, and after a time we begin to feel pretty yucky and separated from the Lord.

Fortunately, God knows this and He has provided a way for us to get fresh spiritual water! How is that? By confession and repentance. The Bible says, *If we confess our sins, He is faithful and just and will forgive us our sins, and purify us from all unrighteousness.* I John 1:9. There is that word again, *purify*! We receive our initial purification from sin, through our salvation in Jesus Christ, and we continue the process of purification through confession and repentance.

No matter how badly you have sinned, no matter how ashamed you may feel, God wants you to enjoy His presence, and He provides a way for you to receive fresh spiritual water. Pray, and confess and repent. He *will* forgive you and welcome you back into His loving embrace.

So every time you sit down to pray, in fact, every time you sin, ask God for forgiveness immediately, and He will forgive you. You will begin your time with Him by removing one of the biggest distractions—unconfessed sin—from your time. Now you can spend time with God and hear His voice!

CONCLUSION:

WHAT IS THE GOAL OF ALL OF THIS? We want to be pure of heart, so that we can see God. The ultimate goal of our spiritual walk is to know God and be with Him. Therefore, we must set aside time from our busy lives and devote our attention to Him. We also should prepare our hearts to receive His attention by purifying ourselves from sin through confession and repentance.

As we walk in our lives, being obedient to God, continually going to Him, and making time for Him, we learn to hear His voice and we indeed become pure of heart, so that we too can *see God!*

REFLECTIONS:

1. In what ways can we be pure of heart, if no man is without sin?
2. What are the two ways we can be pure?
3. How can we see God, if He is a spirit?
4. Can people today still hear the voice of God?
5. Have you ever felt you heard God speaking to you? Describe the experience.
6. If something is really bothering and distracting you during prayer time what is the best way to deal with it?
7. Why is confession of sin so important at the beginning of prayer time?
8. How often do you set aside a block of time, free of distractions, to seek God's presence?

9. What is your favorite time to pray? Favorite place? Why?
10. How can we discern the spirits and know that the thoughts we are hearing are really from God?

CHAPTER 7

JUST WHAT IS A PEACEMAKER?

*Blessed are the peacemakers,
for they shall be called the Children of God
Matt. 5:9*

My teenage years were spent in the 1970s and early 1980s. At that time, whenever I heard the Beatitude, *Blessed are the peacemakers, for they shall be called the children of God*, my thoughts turned to our President, and then former President, Jimmy Carter. He was a good Christian man who negotiated a peace-treaty between Israel and Egypt, and then spent his retirement years running around the world monitoring elections, helping in disasters and building houses for the poor. Surely, Jimmy Carter was exactly the *peacemaker* that Jesus was talking about! As a young man, while I did not agree with Jimmy Carter's politics, I did want to be the type of Christian that he represented.

The problem with this idea of a peacemaker is that it is very limited. Truly, how many of us Christians will be powerful enough, or rich enough, to run about the world setting down opposing parties and helping them reach historic agreements?

Others broaden the definition of *peacemaker* to one who struggles for justice, under the idea that *without justice, there is no peace.* Running with this, whole segments of the Christian community struggle for racial equality,

Michael L. Faber

gather signatures, demonstrate for their favorite causes, all in the name of *justice* and the peace that it will supposedly lead to. Christians have led the charge against slavery, passed child labor laws, supported voting rights for blacks, advocated protection for the unborn, etc. While it is good to struggle for justice, I doubt that this is what Jesus had in mind as He uttered these words during the Sermon on the Mount. We see no follow-up discussion by Christ or Paul or any of the other writers of the New Testament about Christians clamoring for *justice* or advocating for social progress in the secular arena. There is no church history of the earliest Christians picketing Rome, or presenting petitions to Caesar to distribute more food to the poor or to end slavery. We do see individual Christians practicing charity, but is this being a *peacemaker* or some other manifestation of the Christian walk, such as being merciful?

I have made it clear, in this book, that my belief is that Jesus paints a picture in the Beatitudes of what real Christians look like. The Beatitudes are not pie in the sky. They are not a perfect picture of what we cannot attain so we will realize that we need grace, but instead, they describe the type of people we should be when we follow Christ. They are backed up by the entire teaching of Christ, and the witness of the entire Holy Bible, just using different words, perhaps, from what people are used to. Not everyone can be a powerful peacemaking jet-setter, Scripture does not support the idea of a clamoring social activist. What could Jesus have meant when He declared,

Blessed are the peacemakers? More importantly, how can we be the type of a peacemaker that Christ describes?

WHAT IS A PEACEMAKER?

I have a confession to make. No one *really* knows what Jesus meant when He uttered these words. We know this from reading the earliest Christian commentaries on the passage. They all focus on different aspects of what the term might mean and run with it, but there is no real agreement. The same is true today. The problem is, Matthew 5:9 is the *only scripture* where the term *peacemaker* is employed, and there is no follow up instruction or discussion or illustration. Even the companion scripture in Luke 6, which contains a shortened version of the Beatitudes, leaves this one out. Knowing that we cannot understand with certainty what Jesus meant, should we just give up? Not at all. We can use logic, linguistics and comparative bible study to get close, even if we can't hit the bulls eye.

A PEACEMAKER IS ONE WHO PRACTICES EVANGELISM

To begin our quest to understand what it means to be a peacemaker, let's look at the actual word used by Jesus. For those who don't know, the New Testament was written in Greek, even though Jesus spoke Aramaic. At the time the Bible was written, Greek was the common language used all over the Eastern Roman Empire. So scholars must study Greek in order to study the meanings of the New Testament, even though the original words were actually spoken in Aramaic. The Greek word used by Matthew for *peacemaker* as he translated and recorded Jesus' words from the Sermon on the Mount, is the word ειρηνοποιοι. The word ειρηνη literally means *peace*. The second part of the word is ποιοι which literally means *those who make, those who practice, or those who do.*

To *make* peace is to bring peace to a situation where there was no peace. We could use a different word for this, *reconciliation*. While the Bible doesn't say much about causing nations or individuals in conflict with one another to sit down and come to agreement, it says a whole lot about the conflict between man and God, which arose due to sin. The entire theme of the Bible is how God has consistently acted to reconcile Himself to rebellious man, most finally by the offering of His own Son, Jesus to die in our place. Paul states, *All this is from God, who reconciled us to Himself through Christ and gave us the ministry of reconciliation.* 2 Cor. 5:18. He goes on to state, *We are therefore Christ's ambassadors, as though God were making his appeal through us. We implore you on Christ's behalf: Be reconciled to God.* 2 Cor. 5:20.

In other words, the primary way to be a peacemaker is to start with yourself, by making peace with God. You accomplish this by accepting the free gift of salvation through His Son, Jesus Christ. Once you have reconciled yourself to God, you may serve as ambassador of Jesus to implore those around you to themselves make peace with God, through His Son, Jesus Christ! An ambassador's job is to make peace between two sovereign nations; his own and the one to which he is stationed. Let me ask you, *What kind of ambassador would go out of his way to start arguments, engage in fist-fights, and be overly sensitive and difficult to get along with?* Not a very good one! Paul instructed young Timothy about this very point: *Don't have anything to do with foolish and stupid arguments, because you know they produce quarrels. And the Lord's servant must not quarrel, instead he must be kind to everyone, able to teach, not resentful. Those who oppose him, he must gently instruct in the hope that God will grant them repentance leading them to knowledge of the truth…* 2 Tim. 2:23-25. This leads to my second point.

A PEACEMAKER PRACTICES PEACE

To be a good ambassador, one must *practice* peace. The second meaning of the Greek word ποιοι is to practice or carry out an ethical obligation! One who does or practices peace, can do so even in the face of conflict. To be a peace-practitioner is to be a peaceable person, regardless of the actual results. Thinking about this meaning, we do see plenty of scriptural support for *this concept, this understanding* of the term peacemaker.

First of all, we see from the Bible, what a peacemaker/practitioner is not! A peacemaker is *not a troublemaker or a quarrelsome person.* Sometimes to understand more about what something *is* we look first to *what it is not.* The Bible has much to say about troublemakers and quarrelsome people, and it is all bad. One favorite verse of men throughout the world is, *Better to live on a corner of the roof than share a house with a quarrelsome wife.* Proverbs 21:9. Sometimes, after the divorce, all they have left, is the corner of a roof! Not to pick on women, here is one for men. *As charcoal to embers, as wood to fire, so is a quarrelsome man for kindling strife.* Proverbs 26:21. In other words, a quarrelsome person is quick to start a fight. Here is another, *It is to a man's honor to avoid strife, but every fool is quick to quarrel.* Proverbs 20:3. Honorable people keep the peace. Fools find themselves in many arguments. Finally, *Hatred stirs up dissension, but love covers all wrongs.* Proverbs 10:12. Notice the contrast between love and hate. Love makes peace; hatred makes trouble. In a quick review of these few proverbs, we see the Bible portraying quarrelsome people as 1) difficult to live with, 2) constantly in the middle of trouble, 3) haters, and 4) fools. None of these adjectives should apply to the *children of God.* None of these attributes lead to *blessedness.* Certainly, a peacemaker is not a quarrelsome person. They are the opposite.

In the New Testament, Paul uses different words to describe the same type of person, who is definitely not a peacemaker. According to his list of *the acts of the sinful nature"* he includes *"hatred, discord, jealousy, fits of rage, selfish ambition, dissensions, factions, and envy.* Gal. 5:20-21.

Now, we can all picture others who we think are quarrelsome, but rarely do we picture ourselves! We are not quarrelsome are we? If we get into quarrels, it is because we are standing up for what is right. Or we are *contending for the faith.* But when does contending become contention? No one ever quarrels if they believe they are wrong. Why are people quarrelsome? I believe it is because they think themselves to be 100% right, and they are unwilling to allow others to persist in their *erroneous* opinions, whether those opinions be about religion, politics, or a simple fact about anything. Furthermore, quarrelsome people always demand to have the last word about everything. So let's get something straight, *being quarrelsome has nothing to do with whether you are right or wrong. It has everything to do with how you treat other people who differ with you.*

A person who is a peacemaker, does not have to agree with wrong people. He or she does not have to be an appeaser, but there is a way to practice peace, which makes one a peacemaker and not a quarrelsome person. This leads to our next question. How can we practice peace?

STEPS TO BECOMING A PERSON WHO PRACTICES PEACE:

One of the first concepts we must understand is that a person who *practices peace* may not actually obtain peace.

Michael L. Faber

This world is full of conflict, and conflict will remain with us as long as humans walk the earth. This conflict stems from the sin nature. As long as sin persists in the heart of man, so conflict will persist on the face of the earth. Even those who struggle for *justice* in order for there to be peace, will find that if their idea of justice is attained, today's victims will become tomorrow's oppressors. It is unavoidable. Sad to say, we cannot achieve peace on earth even by introducing everyone to Christianity, since Christians have also been fighting amongst themselves and with others since the dawn of our faith. That said, we can have degrees of peace, and we certainly can take steps to avoid contributing to the conflict in the world. When we avoid contributing to the problem, we become peacemakers. We can practice peace, even if full peace is never achieved. Perhaps Paul showed his understanding of this concept when he declared, *As much as depends on you, live peaceably with all men.* Rom. 12:18. He knew that it is impossible to fully avoid conflict, but one certainly can try to avoid unnecessarily contributing to it. How can we do this?

THE FIRST STEP TOWARDS BEING A PEACEMAKER IS TO LEARN TO CONTROL YOUR OWN PASSIONS

We have an old saying, *it takes two to tango.* A tango is a special dance which needs two partners to pull it off. Likewise, many fights and quarrels have two (even if unequal) participants. We can make much peace just by refusing to be part of the problem! In Proverbs, the writer states, *A soft answer turns away wrath, but a harsh word stirs up anger.* Proverbs 15:1. How many young men on the gritty streets of urban America are dead today because they answered a harsh look or word, with an equally harsh retort? How many victims of road rage participated in the conflict with an obscene gesture, after some aggressive move made by the road-rager? Even in my personal relations with individuals with hot tempers or the mentally ill, I find that no matter the provocation, if I answer with anger or violence, it does not stop the situation but only fuels it. You cannot put out a fire by giving it more oxygen, you must smother the fire to make it cease. Likewise, when one is confronted with anger or belligerence a firm but gentle response is what is called for, even when our emotions are urging us to respond in a more aggressive manner. *A peacemaker must learn to control his or her own emotions.*

James, the brother of our Lord Jesus, wrote, *What causes fights and quarrels among you? Don't they come from your desires that battle within you? You want something, but can't get it. You kill and covet, but cannot have what you want. You quarrel and fight.* James 4:1-2. Peacemakers must learn to control their own desires and emotions. It is easy to be a troublemaker. It is natural. Animals fight and devour each other, and people do the same when they listen only to their own primal urges and desires.

Peacemakers need self-control, and this we must work on, and pray for.

THE SECOND STEP TOWARDS BECOMING A PEACEMAKER IS TO WALK IN HUMILITY:

Think about it. How much trouble and strife stems from our constant desire to be Number One! Men fight each other to prove who is strongest. Women backbite and bicker to humiliate other women so that they can rise in the pecking order of women. Nations go to war to prove that they can't be humiliated or disrespected. This is the way of the world. This is the way of the flesh. Followers of Jesus need to find a different way. We follow the path of humility and peace. *Humble yourself before the Lord, and He will lift you up.* James 4:10. Jesus taught about this often. He gave the example of men struggling and elbowing each other for the seat of honor at a banquet. He warned His disciples not to be like this. Instead, *when you are invited, take the lowest place, so that when your host comes, he will say to you, 'Friend, move up to a better place.' Then you will be honored in the presence of all your fellow guests. For everyone who exalts himself, will be humbled, and he who humbles himself will be exalted.* Luke 14:10-11. What does this have to do with peacemaking? When you are proud and haughty, you invite opposition and aggression. When you are humble, others who are themselves aggressive and haughty will not see you as a threat, and thus they will not try to start a conflict with you.

Hey, I thought we were supposed to be peacemakers, not peacekeepers! Christians are not doormats! You might object with these words or thoughts, but the way of Christ is the way of the cross. It is a way of suffering. It is a way of humility. It is a way of peace. If you want to be a hero, a strong man, a Rambo for God, you may do so, but this is not the path of being a peacemaker and you will find yourself in many fights. You will not receive the blessing of being considered a *child of God*. Have you ever noticed how in the movies the action stars are constantly fighting and killing and running? Of course real life is not so dramatic, but the concept is the same. If you present yourself as a strong man who will harbor no insult, you will find yourself in the center of much violence. Win or lose, you will be the opposite of a peacemaker. Peacemakers don't right every wrong, they walk *with all lowliness and gentleness, with long suffering, bearing with one another in love, endeavoring to keep the unity of the Spirit in the bond of peace.* Eph. 4:1-3. Are you getting the picture?

True Christians are humble and meek and gentle. They are patient. They are peacemakers because *they do not cause conflict.* Their demeanor calms people down rather than stirs them up.

THE THIRD STEP OF BEING A PEACEMAKER IS TO LEARN TO SEE THINGS FROM THE OTHER'S POINT OF VIEW

So often we grow up with a Disney movie mentality of ourselves and our opponents. Have you noticed in

Michael L. Faber

Disney cartoons how the heroes and heroines are good people and all beautiful and handsome, and the opponents of the hero or heroine are always wicked people who are ugly and look like monsters? In real life, things are not so black and white. Life is not so black and white. Every person contains within himself a mixture of good and evil motives, a mixture of righteousness and sin. Even bad actors sometimes are trying to do good things through bad methods, and good actors are doing good things with bad motives. We often see ourselves as entirely good and our opponents as entirely evil. A short perusal of the opinion column of the newspaper or the discussion forums on the internet prove this. People don't look at each other as people just trying to do their best by the best means they know how, and sometimes failing. No, they invent caricatures of each other, and dehumanize one another making conflict and violence inevitable.

In the court system, when parties are litigating against one another, often they choose to settle their lawsuits by going to a mediator. A good mediator knows how to defuse the conflict between the parties by helping each party to see the case from the other's point of view. They show each party the weakness in their own case, and the strengths of the other case. Often up to this point, all the parties had in their mind was *I am totally right. The other is totally wrong. I am good, she is evil. I can only win, because the jury will absolutely see my point of view.* The mediator often muddies up the picture by disclosing to the other side, the reality that there are two sides to this conflict, and neither is entirely right. Then the mediator finds the common interests of the parties, and molds a settlement on that.

A mediator is a peacemaker. Peacemakers, whether resolving their own conflicts, or those of others need to learn to see things from the other's point of view. They need to recognize the legitimate concerns and interests of the other. They need to recognize that God loves the other as much as God loves him or her. Paul taught the church at Philippi, *Do nothing out of selfish ambition or vain conceit, but in humility consider others better than yourselves. Each of you should look not only to your own interests, but also to the interests of others.* Phil. 2:3. Notice how Paul didn't say you should totally abandon your own interests, but you need to look at the total picture. Others live in this world also. Not just you. Others have families to feed, honor to maintain, feelings that get hurt. Conflict comes when people look *only* to their own interests, or feel that they are so important, whatever they want outweighs the legitimate needs of others. A peacemaker walks in humility, understanding that he or she is one member of an entire community. Solutions can be found to meet legitimate needs of one party without unnecessarily taking away or burdening the legitimate needs of others. Of course, these solutions can only be found if one is humble enough to even *consider* that others are important enough to even be considered!

When one walks the path of 1) controlling his or her emotions and desires, 2) walking in humility, and 3) seeing problems from others' points of view, one will be making great strides to becoming a peacemaker.

MUST ONE BE AN APPEASER TO BE A PEACEMAKER?

No question ever has an easy answer. Just as most people are basically trying their best to get along with temporary failures, a few people are basically bad. They are cruel. They are overly aggressive and violent. While on an individual level, we try to keep our peace with such people, society as a whole has been given the responsibility by God to deal with such individuals. Paul states that the governing authorities are God's servants, *an agent of wrath to bring punishment on the wrongdoer.* Romans 13:4. Some people are so aggressive, peace can never be made with them, and eventually they must be dealt with by the authorities. There is nothing wrong with the peacemaker turning such a case over to the authorities and cooperating in the investigation and trial of such a bad actor.

Furthermore, governments are charged with the responsibility of protecting their citizens from harm. Sometimes, a government needs to resort to force of arms to protect the legitimate national interests of itself or a weaker nation. Europe learned the hard way that Hitler could not be appeased. He kept demanding more and more, and eventually, Europe had to fight him. This said, and this understood, governments can still be humble and not haughty. They can use gentle words to turn away wrath, or they can make situations worse through harsh rhetoric. They can be quick to start wars or slow. They can consider the interests of other nations and other peoples or only their own. Governments can be peacemakers or warmongers, though even the most peaceful of governments sometimes must fight.

Likewise, peacemaking may not even imply renouncing all forms of violence in private life. Recently, I came across an article describing how a young Asian woman was beaten to death by a group of five women from another ethnic group at a club. The Asian woman brought on the wrath of this other group by either deliberately or accidentally inserting herself into a picture they were taking of themselves. Hundreds of people stood around doing nothing as these five women beat and kicked the young Asian woman to death. Some even took pictures on their cell phones. Peacemaking in this instance required some violence and measured force. Some of the strong men in the crowd should have intervened to protect the Asian woman and remove her from that situation, even if it meant using some violence in her defense. Peacemaking does not imply absolute pacifism or renunciation of all violence. The greater good and the overall peace required the insertion of some violence.

Michael L. Faber

CAN PEACEMAKERS CONTEND FOR THE FAITH?

In the tiny book of Jude, the Apostle writes, *I felt I had to write and urge you to contend for the faith that was once for all entrusted to the saints.* Jude 3. The apostle Paul, as he traveled about, certainly raised his share of controversy, often being beaten and kicked out of town. Where is the peacemaking in all that? It is true that when one considers the ministry of the Apostle Paul, the word *peacemaker* doesn't necessarily spring to mind. Like many spiritual things, there seem to be opposite and conflicting streams of thought. Jesus Himself seemed to admit this when He stated, *Do not suppose that I have come to bring peace on Earth. I did not come to bring peace but a sword. For I have come to turn a man against his father, a daughter against her mother, a daughter-in law-against her mother-in-law, a man's enemies will be the members of his own household.* Matt. 10:34-36.

What Jesus and Jude and Paul were getting at in the above paragraph of teachings is that when you live by the Gospel truth, and proclaim the Gospel truth, you will suffer opposition. Sometimes this opposition will be fierce, and as the martyrs discovered, sometimes it will even be deadly! *In seeking peace, we are not to refrain from speaking and living the truth. For if we cease to speak and act on the truth, we cease to be followers of Christ.* No, we must suffer the inevitable conflict that comes when living out the Gospel. We will discuss this more, in the next chapter discussing the last Beatitude, *Blessed are those who are persecuted because of righteousness.* There are many today, who in seeking to keep the peace in their family, or in their church or in their community, distort the truth, or refuse to speak it out for fear of causing offense. We must be faithful to the truth. For if we will not speak it, no one will.

Like all things, when there seem to be conflicting strains of teaching, that means we are to strike a sensible balance. There is a difference between contending and contention. There is a difference between defending the faith and being argumentative. Much of the discussion up until now has concerned peacemaking when it comes to non-faith-central topics. Individually, if you are a contentious person, a troublemaker, self-centered, and haughty, no one will want to hear the truth of God's gospel from you. When it comes to Gospel truth, we are to be firm, *but gentle.* There are many ways to speak the truth. If you speak the truth in an inappropriate time, place or manner, you will win no one but cause contention. Likewise, *there is a time to keep silent and a time to speak.* Eccl. 3:7. Sometimes this time is in the same conversation. For instance, something might happen that gives you a wonderful opportunity to make a spiritual point. Then the hearer, not wanting to admit the point commences to argue. The point has been made. The hearer heard it and it made an impact. Further argumentation at this point is useless and counterproductive.

Be wise in contending and defending. Be bold, but also be the peacemaker. Be humble yet firm. Make your point. Make your impact. Pay the price if necessary, but do not be argumentative and contentious. Do not unnecessarily stir up trouble, or show lack of wisdom about when it is an appropriate time to speak.

CONCLUSION

Now let's be honest. Few people in this world have the maturity to consider others' needs as important as their own. Few people have the maturity to see their opponents as valuable humans loved by God, instead of dehumanized caricatures. Few people walk in humility or control their emotions. For that reason, there will always be conflict; even in the church. Jesus doesn't demand that His followers actually achieve peace, but He does demand that we practice peace. Peacemaking is not easy. I will make a confession, that as a passionate person, I often struggle with contending for truth, versus being contentious. In our efforts to be peacemakers we will often fail, but as we keep these principles in mind, we will find ourselves in fewer arguments, and we will be making peace more often. We may even mitigate tension as we remember the principles of peacemaking in the middle of an argument that we have foolishly entered into. As Paul says, *As much as depends on you*, live peaceably with all men. Rom. 12:18. Living as a peacemaker will make us better examples of who Jesus is. It will help us in our witnessing to others.

and frankly help us live better and more satisfying lives. Try it. Trust in Jesus. Be a peacemaker. Be considered a *child of God*. What could be better?

REFLECTIONS:
1. How can you be a peacemaker if no one considers your opinion that important?
2. Is participating in struggles for economic justice part of the biblical concept of peacemaking? Why? Why not?
3. How is it possible to be reconciled with God?
4. What kind of personality would a good Ambassador have? What type of personality would make a bad Ambassador?
5. What kinds of attitudes lead to contention and strife?
6. Do you know any contentious people? Are they Christians? How do people treat the ideas presented by contentious people?
7. What are three helpful steps that one can practice in order to become a peacemaker?
8. How can we be a peacemaker without being taken advantage of?
9. How can we be a peacemaker when we know that telling the truth about Jesus causes conflict?
10. Give an example of how you could speak the truth in love while still being gentle, respectful and humble.

CHAPTER 8

CHRISTIANS STAND UP FOR WHAT THEY BELIEVE

Blessed are those who are persecuted because of righteousness, for theirs is the kingdom of heaven.
Matt. 5:10

In 2014, a young woman was sentenced to death and 100 lashes by an Islamic Court in Sudan. She was sentenced to 100 lashes for adultery because she had sex with her husband and became pregnant. She was sentenced to death for apostasy because she would not recant her Christian faith within the three days the Court allowed her. How did such an obviously unjust verdict come to be? Her father was Muslim, he had abandoned the family when she was a young girl and she was raised a Christian by her mother. The law considered her a Muslim because her father was Muslim, even though he did not actually raise her. She married a Christian doctor. Her sister turned her in for *adultery* since Sudan doesn't recognize the marriages between Christians and Muslims. Remember, under Sudanese law, she is a Muslim because of her father. Therefore, because she was not legally married in the eyes of the Sudanese Court, she was guilty of adultery by having sex with a man not recognized as being her husband. Muslims who become Christians are deemed guilty of apostasy and are sentenced to death. Since she was legally considered a Muslim, she was guilty of apostasy, but the Court in its leniency gave her three days to come to her senses and renounce her Christian faith. She refused to renounce Jesus, and therefore she was sentenced to death. Her name is Meriam Yahya. Due to her pregnancy, the sentence was delayed. Due to international pressure, she was eventually freed and immigrated to the United States on a special visa, but she could not have known that when she made her stand for Jesus. She truly is a hero of the faith! Would we have made the same decision?

In 2014, thirty-three Christians were executed in North Korea for the crime of setting up home churches in that repressive Communist nation, which clings to atheism as its official dogma. They were caught and executed for cooperating with South Korean missionary, Kim Jung Wook. Korean Christians are no strangers to religious persecution. Internet reports currently speak of over 100,000 Christians in North Korean labor camps. Even the Korean Protestant church began in blood. In 1866, Missionary Robert J. Thomas accompanied an armed American Trading Boat as a translator. He carried 500 Chinese Bibles with him to handout to the Korean Christians (Catholics) who did not possess the scriptures. At that time literate Koreans could read Chinese characters. This trading mission was not welcomed by the government of Korea, and orders were dispatched to sink the ship and kill all those on board. When the boat came under attack, Rev. Thomas began throwing the Bibles to the people on shore crying out, *Jesus, Jesus*. When it came time for his execution, he handed the executioner his last Bible. The executioner hesitated but carried out his duty. He took the Bible, and since he could not read, used the pages as wallpaper for his house. Later generations learned to read, and began reading the *wallpaper* and gave their lives to Christ. The Executioner's house became the first house church in North Korea! Later revivals swept over the Korean peninsula and while still under heavy persecution in the North, the Christian Faith has been embraced by the majority of South Koreans.

In 2014, approximately 276 girls were kidnapped from their school in northern Nigeria by Muslim extremists, a group called Boko Haram. They were given the choice of becoming Muslims and being married off, or retaining their Christian faith and being sold off as slaves or prostitutes. Some of the girls converted to the Muslim faith so things would go easier on them. Others maintained their faith in Christ, and as of the time this book was published, have still not been found.

In 2014, 75-year-old Jesuit Father Frans van der Lugt, who had worked in Syria since 1966, declined suggestions to leave that war-torn nation because he wanted to help Syria's suffering civilians, *Christians and Muslims -- anyone in need,* He issued press conferences appealing to the world to help the citizens of Homs who were suffering under a government blockade. In April, 2014, armed men beat him up and put two bullets in his head. We don't know if his killers were Muslim extremists or Government agents, who saw him as supporting the rebellion through his charity work.

As Jesus preached His Beatitudes, during the Sermon on the Mount, he uttered the words, *Blessed are those who are persecuted because of righteousness, for theirs is the kingdom of heaven.* Matt. 5:10. This is the only Beatitude that he went on to explain further. He continued in verses 11-12, with the words, *Blessed are you when people insult you, persecute you and falsely say all kinds of evil against you because of me. Rejoice and be glad, because great is your reward in heaven, for in the same way they persecuted the prophets who were before you.*

As suggested by Jesus, **Christians stand up for what they believe in.** When you believe in something and are firm about it, you are going to generate opposition, and even persecution. Christians have been persecuted from the earliest days of the faith. They were persecuted by the Jews, the Romans and then by Islam. They have been persecuted by each other, and sometimes even by the Church. They have been killed for their faith in lands to which they traveled to preach the faith. They have been slaughtered by the thousands in Japan, Korea, and Vietnam. In the 20th Century, they have been persecuted by the Nazis, the Communists, and most recently by Muslim extremists.

Michael L. Faber

PERSECUTION COMES IN MANY FORMS:

In my initial examples, Christians were killed, threatened with death or slavery for either not renouncing their faith, or for simply living it out. Some Christians die because they are given a choice to recant and fail to do so. Some die simply because they are a hated minority, and the majority is carrying out some type of ethnic cleansing. Some are persecuted because, even though being a Christian is not illegal, the practice of Christian worship and evangelism is highly regulated, and Christians are compelled to get on the wrong side of the law if they want to go to church, study the Bible, or evangelize. Some are killed because in the practice of their faith, they speak out for the disadvantaged or neglected, and get on the wrong side of powerful opposition. Still others are simply slandered, hated, fired, fined or punished because what they stand for, or say, is loathsome to someone else with power.

The woman in Sudan was given a stark choice. *Renounce your faith or die.* She chose faith. Seldom in this world are we given such a clear choice, but history is littered with corpses of martyrs who stood firm in such a test. During the first three hundred years of Christianity, various Emperors of Rome tried to persecute Christians in this manner. Christians were told to hand over their holy books, stop worshiping and swear oaths to the Roman gods. If they refused, they were interrogated and given many chances to renounce their faith in Jesus so they could live. Sometimes their family came to the trial and pled with them to make the oath or put the pagan sacrifice on the altar so they could return home in safety. Due to their faith, these Christians stood firm. Often they were tortured and imprisoned over many days or months and given many chances to change their mind. Only those who persisted were killed. To them, standing firm for Jesus was sharing in His suffering, and they were not looking for the pleasures of this life, but for the heavenly kingdom to come.

From the late 1500s to the early 1600s many thousands of Japanese Christians were given the choice to renounce their faith or die. The same thing happened in Vietnam during the 1830s. The Vatican estimates that between 130,000 and 300,000 Christians were put to death in Vietnam during this time. This, *recant or die* is the most extreme form of persecution, and through the ages, faithful Christians have proven that such tactics cannot destroy Christianity. If anything, such persecution makes the Church stronger, because it forces weak-willed and luke-warm Christians to step up their faith, or quit. In 197 A.D., Tertullian declared, *The blood of the martyrs is the seed of the church.*

In North Korea, Christians were executed for simply trying to worship. We have no record of any trials where the Communists sought to make them give up their beliefs, they were simply killed for doing what was forbidden, which in this case was gathering together to worship God. Again, our history shows that Christians will continue to meet, even when forbidden to do so. They will meet despite threats of imprisonment or death. In places like Vietnam and North Korea, where Christians were only allowed to worship at a few state-sanctioned official churches which were monitored and controlled by the government, Christians continued to meet in homes and fields, wherever they could. Thinking about such people should put shame to Western Christians. Here in the U.S. while 95% claim to believe in God, fewer than 35% attend worship regularly. In Western Europe and Canada, the numbers are even lower. How many of us would go to church if we thought we might be arrested?

In 1993, I visited some unregistered home churches in Ho Chi Minh City, Vietnam. As I stood there, in that place, the feeling of fear was palpable. The sound of a motorbike approaching could have meant police, fines and jail for those present. I marveled at the joy these people had in spite of this official persecution. While we felt the fear, we also felt the Holy Spirit in power! They asked me to teach them something, and I truthfully declared, *I have nothing to teach you. You are teaching me.* In the West, we wonder if we should skip worship to attend sporting events, BBQs or to catch some extra sleep. Often our choice of church attendance is driven by what we feel is going to give us maximum pleasure. Never does attending church bring to our minds the prospect or imprisonment or death.

The fate of the 276 kidnapped school girls is also a lesser but still severe form of persecution. All of these girls were kidnapped against their will, but they had the *choice* of renouncing their faith and facing perhaps an easier life, or holding firm to their faith and suffering more severe persecution; in this case slavery. This is a very severe example of the type of choice faced by many Christians today. Hold fast to the faith, or compromise and give in, so that life will be easier. How often are we presented with the choice of compromising our beliefs so that things will go better for us? We may not be told, *Become a Muslim or be a slave* but we might be told, *Keep your mouth shut about this moral issue or that, if you want to get along or advance in this company.* Not all forms of persecution come with the threat of death or slavery. Jesus made it clear that some persecution is as simple as being slandered, hated and insulted. Other types of persecution may involve economic penalties.

In the United States, today, CEOs, TV figures and sports action heroes are losing their jobs for saying that God considers the practice of homosexuality a sin. A member of the now famous Duck Dynasty reality show initially lost his job, and later was denounced by the media and opinion makers, for merely quoting what the Bible has to say about the topic. The CEO of Mozilla was pressured out of his job because he had donated money six years earlier to a California ballot proposition to keep marriage only between a man and a woman. Homosexuality is the hot topic at the time this book is being written, but in the past, individuals have been persecuted for opposing slavery or preaching this doctrine or that. Being faithful to Christ is *more than just saying that you believe in Him as opposed to some alternate Deity or none at all.* It also includes standing up for the teachings of the faith. Many times these teachings may be quite unpopular with non-Christians and nominal Christians. Notice that while, Jesus said we would suffer all kinds of things for his *Name's sake*, the blessed ones would be persecuted *because of righteousness.*

Speaking the truth in love will necessarily generate opposition. In the current political environment of the United States, speaking the truth about sexual purity, and marriage, and the protection of the unborn will often deny politicians the ability to get elected, and more and more will bring economic consequences to those who depend on government goodwill or public opinion for their livelihood.

In Luke's companion Sermon, Blessings and Woes, Jesus fleshes this out a little more. He states, *Blessed are you when men hate you, when they exclude you and insult you and reject your name as evil, because of the Son of Man.* Lk. 6:22. He goes on to declare, *Woe to you when all men speak well of you, for that is how their fathers treated the false prophets.* Lk. 6:26. Unfortunately, being true to the Gospel and to the authentic teaching of God's Word will often generate public opposition. Why? Because God often teaches that we must sacrifice our individual pursuit of gratification for the well-being of others. He teaches that we must discipline and restrain our sexual desires and appetites. He teaches that there is an absolute truth, and because of this, others are living a lie. All of these ideas are repulsive to the flesh, and to those who live by the flesh and not the spirit. When Christians proclaim these ideas they are necessarily rebuked and looked down upon by the rest of society which does not value the Word of God as absolute truth. Sometimes, the result is simply that the individual Christian is excluded or looked down upon as an ignorant uneducated *hater*. Sometimes, when enough Christians stand together, they become a threat to the dominant power, and the dominant power may act to persecute Christianity as a whole. On the other hand, Christians must be careful not to water down, or explain away, or distance themselves from essential Christian truth, just because they are trying to *be relevant* to this generation, or even worse to avoid persecution. Remember what Jesus said, *Woe to you when all men speak well of you, for this is how their fathers treated the false prophets.* For a true believer, some opposition is unavoidable. In the end, we must please God and not man.

In my last example, we don't know if Fr. Frans van der Lugt was killed by extremists simply because he was a Catholic priest, or if he was killed by the Syrian government for publicly advocating the humanitarian cause of the citizens of Homs. Either way, he is blessed. He is blessed because he was killed either for simply being a Christian, or he was killed for *acting like a Christian!* Remember our last chapter about peacemakers? Father Frans van der Lugt was being a peacemaker by placing himself in a position of danger and advocating for the unfortunate people of

Michael L. Faber

Homs who did not have a voice of their own. *Speak up for those who cannot speak for themselves, for the rights of all who are destitute. Speak up and judge fairly; defend the rights of the poor and the needy.* Prov. 31:8-9. Do not think for a second that one can act so without a cost. If you speak up for those who have no power, and defend the rights of the poor and needy, you will infuriate the strong and the powerful. They will probably strike back.

In the 1980s missionaries, priests and nuns were often raped and murdered in Central America because they stood side by side with the poor members of their churches against the powerful landowning interests that controlled the governments. These included Archbishop Oscar Romero, six Jesuits, four US Protestant missionaries, several Mary Knoll sisters, just in El Salvador alone, during the Civil War in the 1980s.

Even in the United States today, try to open a homeless ministry in your neighborhood and see what happens. While everyone will give lip-service to helping the poor, they will not like it if you start bringing poor people into your neighborhood. You will find that complaints are filed against you, the police will show up and the city will try to shut you down. Trying to *be Jesus* to the poor and the downtrodden will come with a cost.

In our earlier chapter, we discussed what it meant for Christians to act as peacemakers. We determined that while we must live at peace as much as we are able, and not let our own fleshly desires be the cause of conflict, when we stand up for the essence of truth some conflict will inevitably occur. This last Beatitude discusses where the rubber really meets the road. While we are meek, and poor of spirit, and practice peace, we also mourn sin, we act to preserve justice and righteousness, we defend the poor and the needy, and we are firm in our convictions. This is so, even if it means personal unpopularity, persecution or even death. To be real Christians, and real people of God, we also need to be courageous.

HOW DOES BEING PERSECUTED MAKE YOU BLESSED?

As shown in the first chapter, to be blessed means to be happy or given a special favor by God. It makes sense that those who are merciful or humble or peacemaking find happiness by attaining peace in their lives and avoiding the rat-race. But how can being persecuted, ridiculed, oppressed or even killed lead to blessedness, or happiness?

I don't believe that the actual persecution itself is a happy time. Of course it is no fun to endure pain and punishment. Where the happiness comes is before and after the persecution. Before the persecution, a person who stands up for what is right, what is true, and what is just, enjoys *a meaningful life*. This gets down to the question of whether we want the longest life or the most meaningful life. People that stand up for righteousness in the face of evil are accomplishing something. They are standing for something. They are making a difference! Due to this, they live in great joy and blessedness. When the time of persecution comes, it is possible that their earthly life may be shortened or made more difficult, but then they receive the heavenly blessing from God! We don't know how this will necessarily look, but we do know that it is promised by our Lord Jesus Christ, so that we who live faithfully can count on it!

DO NOT SEEK OUT PERSECUTION

Like all things, we must learn to live in balance. During the Great Persecution of Rome, prior to the reign of Constantine, many Christians who tried to mind their own business were caught up in the judicial system and put to the test. Often while the trials and interrogations were going on in some public space, other Christians would hear about it and show up and announce they too were Christians, and the government complied by having them executed along with the initial martyrs. The Early Church did not approve of these latter volunteer martyrs and some even accused them of not being Christians at all. As I discussed in my last chapter on peacemaking, there is a way of proclaiming the truth in a gentle loving manner which may provoke some opposition, and there is a way of proclaiming the truth in a rude, insensitive and abrasive manner which will generate lots of opposition both to oneself, and the truth that one is trying to proclaim.

Likewise, an individual Christian may conduct himself in a faithful and true, humble and loving fashion and still be persecuted; or an individual can act in a haughty, proud and abrasive manner, all but daring the persecutor to strike him down. This latter way is not the way of Jesus. At all times, one must practice peace, even while boldly standing for the truth. In his discussion about suffering for doing good works, Peter declares that if we do good, most of the time we will not be harmed. I Pet. 3:13, *But even if you should suffer for doing what is right, you are blessed!* I Pet. 3:14. He counsels Christians to be courageous and not to be frightened, but he adds the instruction, *Always be prepared to give an answer to everyone who asks you to give the reason for the hope that you have. But do so this with gentleness and respect, keeping a clear conscience, so that those who speak maliciously against your good behavior in Christ may be ashamed of their slander.* I Pet. 3:15.

We can do good works in a fashion that raises hackles, offends sensibilities, and makes persecution all but certain, or we can do good works in a way that is respectful and loving, designed to bring the potential persecutor from where he is, to the place where God wants him to be. Yes, persecution may result even when we are being respectful and loving, but in that case it is persecution that could not be avoided, not persecution that was caused by rudeness and insensitivity.

During the Great Persecution of Rome, there were young men who would run up to officials who were performing sacrifices as part of their official duties, and hit the officials, knock over the altar and denounce them in the middle of the ceremony. These young men were also executed. Peter declared, *It is better if it is God's will to suffer for doing good than for doing evil.* I Pet. 3:17. Were these young men persecuted for righteousness or for being jerks? We should not bring persecution upon ourselves through boorish behavior.

PERSECUTION FOR DISOBEYING THE LAW

In almost every instance of persecution, Christians are lawfully convicted of breaking the law of the land, and receive for themselves the punishment the law demands. This is true, whether the law is just or not. Even Meriam Yahya was convicted in a court of law according to the laws of the land. In Roman times, Christians were not persecuted for simply *being Christian*. They were persecuted for attending worship services, not turning over holy books, or refusing to offer sacrifices to the Roman gods. Caesar had declared the law. Christians had the option to obey these laws and remain unmolested or disobeying them and suffering punishment. Likewise, during the persecution of the Japanese and Vietnamese Christians, it was not that the government hated Jesus Christ *per se*; these rulers just feared that those who followed the religions of the West would operate as a Fifth Column and perhaps usher in Western colonialism. The Emperors who tried to wipe out Christianity did not do so because they worshiped the devil, but because they felt it was in the best interests of their nation to oppose this foreign religion. Even in the U.S., much persecution of Christian faithful is done in the name of science, civil liberty, or good zoning. Some people of good will feel Christianity stands in the way of gays and lesbians achieving the right to marry, so they attack Christianity on the internet and call Christians *haters*. In other instances, where Christians receive punishment for violation of such things as zoning and immigration laws, the laws in and of themselves have nothing to do with religion. Christians fall afoul of these laws when trying to *act like Christians*. When they feed the homeless in a park, or conduct a Bible study in their homes, or shelter an illegal alien fleeing persecution in Central America, they are acting contrary to law. In every instance, the persecuting power can and does claim that what it is doing is in the public interest. The Christians on the other hand tend to say something like, *We must obey God and not man.*

The Bible actually commands Christians to follow the law. Paul states, *Everyone must submit himself to the governing authorities, for there is no authority except that which God has established.* Rom. 13:1. Paul commands Christians to pay taxes and give due honor to government officials because *He is God's servant, an agent of wrath to bring punishment on the wrongdoer.* Rom. 13:4. For this reason, Christians can declare with good reason that it is a sin to drive too fast, even though the Bible says nothing about driving. It is a sin to drive too fast because lawful government has made driving too fast illegal, and to break the law is to defy the authority established by God to keep the public order. Therefore, driving too fast is a sin.

Michael L. Faber

The problem results when the established authority establishes laws that are directly contrary to the laws of God. While Christians can rightfully say, that it is a sin to break any secular law that does *not* contradict the clear word of God, it *is* a sin to follow secular laws which break God's law. A captain cannot legally tell his soldiers to disobey the general. Likewise, while Christians must obey all lawful secular authority, we cannot do so if secular authority commands us to sin against God. God established the power of the secular authority, and thus outranks it. If there is a conflict, God must be obeyed. During the Nazi times, people were required to report and turn in Jews so that they could be exterminated in the Death Camps. Some Christians blindly followed these laws under the authority of Romans 13, but the more discerning and courageous Christians refused to obey these laws, and instead hid the Jews at their own peril. The same was true for people who ran the under-ground railroad in the mid-1800s. They illegally helped slaves escape their masters in violation of both State and Federal laws.

Communist countries made laws prohibiting Christians from sharing the gospel with others, and prohibiting them from possessing Bibles or attending meetings anywhere but at State sanctioned churches. Christians rightfully violated these laws, because they were directly contrary to what the word of God required of them. It is the essence of the Christian Faith to confess Christ as Savior and Lord, to worship no God but Yahweh, to share the gospel with others, and to meet together for worship, Bible study and prayer. The Bible is full of stories of young men who stood up to maintain their faith despite secular laws forbidding it. Think of Daniel, think of Shadrach, Meshach and Abednego. Think of the Jews who died for not eating pork as demanded of them, as recounted in the book of Maccabees. Likewise, Stephen went to his death, Peter and John were imprisoned, Paul continued to preach despite being persecuted, beaten and imprisoned. Now, if they were caught, they received whatever punishment the law demanded, because legally they were guilty. But they counted it joy to be persecuted for their faith.

One can rightfully say that we cannot make exceptions in the law simply because of one's religious faith. The law needs to apply equally to everyone regardless of their personal beliefs. At the same time, to be humane, government should avoid passing laws that infringe on an individual's conscience and basic desire to worship as he chooses. For laws that do not specifically prohibit one from practicing his religion, good governance cannot allow an individual veto, simply because the individual decides that the law violates some minor tenet of his or her own religion. But in spite of this, true Christians may still need to disobey the law from time to time to be who they are called to be, and this may entail being forced to pay the penalty the law requires. A good example of this conflict might be where one is compelled by zoning laws not to feed the homeless, or not to have a Bible study in one's house. Due to American constitutional law, sometimes these *unjust laws* fall upon later court review as being in violation of the First Amendment and sometimes they don't. But Christians of good conscience need to decide if they are going to obey the law, or stand for a higher principle instead. If they choose to stand for the higher principle they must be willing to pay the price. There have been many unjust laws changed in the course of human history, only after brave people refused to obey them to their own personal detriment.

Sometimes all Christians may not agree with the persecuted. The American Civil Rights movement comes to mind. Many Christians of goodwill disagreed with the tactics and behavior of Martin Luther King Jr. as he defied civil authority in the name of God for equal treatment of black people. Other Christians felt he was sinning by stirring up trouble and disobeying lawful authority, and that change should come through political means not civil disobedience. History has judged that Martin Luther King, Jr. was correct in his assessment, but often while things are happening on the ground, the issues are not clear. Christians need to learn to walk by the Spirit in discerning when to stand firm, and when to back down.

TRUE CHRISTIANS STAND UP FOR WHAT THEY BELIEVE IN

While Christians are called to be people of peace, they are also called to be people of courage. We understand that the ultimate authority in the universe is God, and to obey God and be faithful to God is our highest calling. While we are called to live at peace with all men as much as it depends on us, at the same time we are called to shine the light of Christ to all men in a gentle and respectful manner. We are called not only to be the light of the world, but the salt of the earth. We are called to practice peace and to do justice, as we proclaim the truth. When we do these things, we will frequently fall afoul of the institutions of man, since man is sinful. We do not seek out persecution, but we will faithfully stand in the face of it, if need be.

By their very nature, those who are being persecuted for righteousness are often in violation of the law. They are violating laws of the government, or social laws of society. By standing for what is absolutely true and right, Christians may fall afoul of the government or of society, especially if society and its laws are corrupt. Heroic Christians and people of God will do so whatever the cost. *Blessed are those who are persecuted because of righteousness, for theirs is the kingdom of heaven.*

REFLECTIONS
1. How can suffering for righteousness lead an individual to be happy or blessed?
2. What does this kind of blessedness look like?
3. Can you describe some incident in your life where you felt you needed to disobey the law for the greater good?

4. Have you ever been persecuted for your faith? What form did that persecution take?
5. Have you ever decided to compromise your walk with Christ in order to avoid persecution? What happened? Would you make the same decision again?
6. Should Christians frequently perform acts of Civil Disobedience in order to *change the law?* What other principles might this course of action conflict with?
7. How much of your religious freedom would you be willing to give up before you would stand up even in the face of imprisonment or death?
8. If you were in a situation where the authorities told you *Renounce Jesus or die!*, What would be the harm in renouncing Jesus until you were freed from their grasp and then going home and confessing and asking for forgiveness?
9. If the Church were persecuted in your home country, what would be the likely result?

CONCLUSION

We started this journey asking, what does Jesus say we need to do to be happy? We found that He answered this question by saying that we need to be Kingdom People, and Kingdom People are described in the Beatitudes. We looked at each Beatitude in some depth and found that while sometimes they seem to be contrary to *common sense* or the *way things are naturally done,* they did make sense at a deeper level and lead to a greater blessedness over a longer haul than offered by the direct approach of simply seizing or doing whatever you think will make you happy in the moment.

Of course, if we believe in God and the eternal life only He offers, then the answer is clear that in order to achieve the maximum amount of happiness over the greatest amount of time (in this case eternity) we need to do what God requires of us in this life to attain eternal life.

We begin our quest for eternal life by placing our faith in Jesus Christ as Lord and Savior. *For God so loved the world that he gave his one and only Son, that whoever believes in him shall not perish but have eternal life.* John 3:16 (NIV). Jesus instructed His apostles to *make disciples of all nations, baptizing them in the name of the Father, and of the Son and of the Holy Spirit, and teaching them to obey everything I have commanded you.* Matt. 28:19-20.

We enter the Kingdom of God, and the promised eternal life by placing our faith in Christ and then getting baptized. We live there by obeying Christ. Part of our obedience is being the type of people He wants us to be. He describes this type of person in the Beatitudes and the rest of the Gospels, and Paul, Peter and John flesh it out even further in the New Testament. In this book, we have taken a short glance at the Beatitudes.

If you have yet to place your faith in Christ, but feel the call to do so now, you may begin your Kingdom Journey by simply praying the below prayer:

Jesus. I trust in you. I am sorry for the sin that I have committed in my life. Please forgive Me. Thank you for dying for me so that I might live. I accept your free gift of salvation. Please come into my life as Lord and Master and guide me in the way you want me to live. I want to be your child, and I want to please you. Amen.

Congratulations! If you prayed that prayer and meant it, you are a new child of God and a new citizen of the Kingdom of God. You have taken the first step in a life long journey. Now, secure yourself a Bible and begin reading it. Find a Church that will walk along side you in your faith journey, guide you and teach you, and make preparations to get baptized in the Name of the Father, the Son and the Holy Spirit. You have a long exciting spiritual journey ahead of you as you discover God's will through His word, and attempt to put it into practice with the assistance of the Holy Spirit! Blessings to you!

ACKNOWLEDGMENTS

I wish to acknowledge the contribution of Dr. Priscilla Turner who assisted me by proof reading my manuscript and providing critique on the substance of the manuscript from time to time which helped me sharpen my argument. Any remaining errors are my own, since I confess, I tinkered with the manuscript after her edits.

I also wish to give my thanks to Julie Williams who designed my book cover and provided technical expertise to get my book from manuscript form into the proper formats for publishing both in print and electronically.

Special thanks are also due to Pastor Philip Khanh Trinh and Grace Presbyterian Church in Sacramento, CA, for giving me a forum to preach once a month and to express the ideas contained in this book. You may hear these chapters being preached in English and translated into Vietnamese by going to www.vietchristian.com/sermons and navigating to my name.

I wish to thank Pastor Gabriel Muppidi who has faithfully translated my last several books (*Meditations on the Lord's Prayer*, and *Seven Words of Jesus from the Cross*) and now this one into the Telugu language for distribution to home church pastors and Christian leaders in India.

Further thanks to my mother, Elaine Faber, and my wife, Mai Faber, for encouraging me to write and publish.

Finally, all praise to our Lord Jesus Christ for inspiring me to write these works and making it possible for them to be distributed in English, Telugu and Vietnamese to various peoples of the world.

ABOUT THE AUTHOR:
MICHAEL L. FABER

There is nothing great or special about the author that would make you want to read this book unless, of course, you know him personally and that is why you are looking at it. The words and ideas of this book must stand on their own. Not because Michael L. Faber taught them, but because they are about Jesus…and He is great.

Michael L. Faber has been a lay preacher in various Baptist, Presbyterian and Charismatic churches since 1993. He graduated from Fuller Seminary with a Master's Degree in Bible and Theology in 2012, where he learned Greek and Hebrew and the art of textual criticism. He is also a practicing California Attorney.

During his ministry, he has developed a heart for the Vietnamese people. He often preaches at Vietnamese churches (in English), retirement homes and youth groups. His sermons are often translated contemporaneously by the Vietnamese pastors, so the young people can hear the sermons in English and the older people can hear them in their native language, Vietnamese. Through his last book, *Meditations on the Lord's Prayer*, he gained a connection with India as well. His previous books have been translated to Telugu and distributed in South East India and they are also being translated into Vietnamese for distribution to the Vietnamese people in Vietnam and overseas.

Michael L. Faber's sermons can be heard online at www.vietchristian.com/sermon. He would love to hear from you. You may contact him at mfaber@elkgrove.net. You may order more copies of this book by e-mail or going to the publisher website at www.elkgrovepublications.com. Books may also be ordered in print or e-book format on Amazon.

OTHER BOOKS BY MICHAEL L. FABER

Meditations on the Lords Prayer (2013)

Seven Words of Jesus from the Cross (2013)

www.ingramcontent.com/pod-product-compliance
Lightning Source LLC
Chambersburg PA
CBHW030326080526
44584CB00012B/730